ESSENTIALS OF
Existential
Phenomenological
Research

Essentials of Qualitative Methods Series

Essentials of Autoethnography
Christopher N. Poulos

Essentials of Consensual Qualitative Research
Clara E. Hill and Sarah Knox

Essentials of Conversation Analysis
Alexa Hepburn and Jonathan Potter

Essentials of Critical-Constructivist Grounded Theory Research
Heidi M. Levitt

Essentials of Critical Participatory Action Research
Michelle Fine and María Elena Torre

Essentials of Descriptive-Interpretive Qualitative Research: A Generic Approach
Robert Elliott and Ladislav Timulak

Essentials of Discursive Psychology
Linda M. McMullen

Essentials of Existential Phenomenological Research
Scott D. Churchill

Essentials of Ideal-Type Analysis: A Qualitative Approach to Constructing Typologies
Emily Stapley, Sally O'Keeffe, and Nick Midgley

Essentials of Interpretative Phenomenological Analysis
Jonathan A. Smith and Isabella E. Nizza

Essentials of Narrative Analysis
Ruthellen Josselson and Phillip L. Hammack

Essentials of Thematic Analysis
Gareth Terry and Nikki Hayfield

ESSENTIALS OF

Existential Phenomenological Research

Scott D. Churchill

 AMERICAN PSYCHOLOGICAL ASSOCIATION

Published by
American Psychological Association
750 First Street, NE
Washington, DC 20002
https://www.apa.org

Order Department
https://www.apa.org/pubs/books
order@apa.org

In the U.K., Europe, Africa, and the Middle East, copies may be ordered from Eurospan
https://www.eurospanbookstore.com/apa
info@eurospangroup.com

Typeset in Charter and Interstate by Circle Graphics, Inc., Reisterstown, MD

Printer: Gasch Printing, Odenton, MD
Cover Designer: Anne C. Kerns, Anne Likes Red, Inc., Silver Spring, MD

Library of Congress Cataloging-in-Publication Data

Names: Churchill, Scott D. (Scott Demane), author.
Title: Essentials of existential phenomenological research / by Scott D. Churchill.
Description: Washington, DC : American Psychological Association, [2022] |
  Series: Essentials of qualitative methods series | Includes bibliographical references
  and index.
Identifiers: LCCN 2021006223 (print) | LCCN 2021006224 (ebook) |
  ISBN 9781433835711 (paperback) | ISBN 9781433835728 (ebook)
Subjects: LCSH: Existential psychology—Research—Methodology. |
  Phenomenological psychology—Research—Methodology. | Existential
  phenomenology. | Qualitative research—Methodology. | Psychology—Methodology.
Classification: LCC BF204.5 .C48 2022 (print) | LCC BF204.5 (ebook) |
  DDC 150.19/2—dc23
LC record available at https://lccn.loc.gov/2021006223
LC ebook record available at https://lccn.loc.gov/2021006224

https://doi.org/10.1037/0000257-000

Printed in the United States of America

10 9 8 7 6 5 4 3 2 1

Contents

Series Foreword—Clara E. Hill and Sarah Knox   *vii*

1. **Conceptual Foundations of Existential Phenomenological Research**   **3**
   The "Human Science" Approach as a Way of Seeing   *5*
   What Is the Key Insight of Existential Phenomenology?   *10*
   Summary   *17*

2. **Getting Started: Selecting an Experience to Study**   **21**
   Formulating a Research Question   *22*
   Summary   *31*

3. **Collecting the Data**   **33**
   Attending to Ethical Considerations   *33*
   Selecting Participants   *35*
   Developing an Experiential "Approach" to Data Collection   *36*
   Data-Generating Activities   *37*
   Summary   *46*

4. **First Phase of Data Analysis: Focusing on Moments Within the Whole**   **47**
   Doing Psychology Phenomenologically   *48*
   Mentoring EPR in the Classroom: Training the Research Team   *59*
   Summary   *60*

5. **Second Phase of Data Analysis: Comprehensive Synthesis**   **61**
   Individual Structural Description: A Comprehensive Synthesis   *62*
   General Structural Description: The Intuition of Essential Meaning   *66*
   Summary   *71*

6. Writing the Research Report   **73**
Introduction Section   *74*
Method Section   *74*
Results Section   *76*
Discussion Section   *77*
Summary   *77*

7. Conclusions   **79**
The Place of Phenomenology Within the Qualitative Tradition   *80*
Achieving Methodological Integrity   *81*
Strengths, Limitations, and Future Directions   *85*

Appendix: Exemplar Studies (1971–2020)   *89*
References   *91*
Index   *101*
About the Author   *107*
About the Series Editors   *109*

Series Foreword

Qualitative approaches have become accepted and indeed embraced as empirical methods within the social sciences, as scholars have realized that many of the phenomena in which we are interested are complex and require deep inner reflection and equally penetrating examination. Quantitative approaches often cannot capture such phenomena well through their standard methods (e.g., self-report measures), so qualitative designs using interviews and other in-depth data-gathering procedures offer exciting, nimble, and useful research approaches.

Indeed, the number and variety of qualitative approaches that have been developed is remarkable. We remember Bill Stiles saying (quoting Chairman Mao) at one meeting about methods, "Let a hundred flowers bloom," indicating that there are many appropriate methods for addressing research questions. In this series, we celebrate this diversity (hence, the cover design of flowers).

The question for many of us, though, has been how to decide among approaches and how to learn the different methods. Many prior descriptions of the various qualitative methods have not provided clear enough descriptions of the methods, making it difficult for novice researchers to learn how to use them. Thus, those interested in learning about and pursuing qualitative research need crisp and thorough descriptions of these approaches, with lots of examples to illustrate the method so that readers can grasp how to use the methods.

The purpose of this series of books, then, is to present a range of qualitative approaches that seemed most exciting and illustrative of the range of methods appropriate for social science research. We asked leading experts in qualitative methods to contribute to the series, and we were delighted that they accepted our invitation. Through this series, readers have the opportunity to learn qualitative research methods from those who developed the methods and/or who have been using them successfully for years.

We asked the authors of each book to provide context for the method, including a rationale, situating the method within the qualitative tradition, describing the method's philosophical and epistemological background, and noting the key features of the method. We then asked them to describe in detail the steps of the method, including the research team, sampling, biases and expectations, data collection, data analysis, and variations on the method. We also asked authors to provide tips for the research process and for writing a manuscript emerging from a study that used the method. Finally, we asked authors to reflect on the methodological integrity of the approach, along with the benefits and limitations of the particular method.

This series of books can be used in several different ways. Instructors teaching courses in qualitative research could use the whole series, presenting one method at a time to expose students to a range of qualitative methods. Alternatively, instructors could choose to focus on just a few approaches, as depicted in specific books, supplementing the books with examples from studies that have been published using the approaches, and providing experiential exercises to help students get started using the approaches.

In this book, Scott D. Churchill describes existential phenomenological research (EPR), a philosophy-based qualitative method that focuses on how we understand the nature of our subject matter, as well as how we access that subject matter. The data of EPR focus on how individuals are "thrown into" situations in life and how, within those situations, individuals find "avenues of choice." Researchers access such phenomena via empathy, intuition, or "listening with the third ear." As central features of EPR, Churchill notes the following: an evidence-based method examining individuals' psychological lives, researchers who "bring themselves to the evidence," reliance on first-person descriptions of experience and researchers' reflections on those experiences, and researchers' cultivation of both sensitivity to meaning and a sense of empathy, curiosity, and wonder in human experience.

—*Clara E. Hill and Sarah Knox*

ESSENTIALS OF

Existential
Phenomenological
Research

1 CONCEPTUAL FOUNDATIONS OF EXISTENTIAL PHENOMENOLOGICAL RESEARCH

There are two general kinds of research where existential phenomenological methods are particularly useful. The first application is when one is seeking knowledge about what constitutes certain "kinds" of experiences, such as the various emotions. In these cases, we find ourselves asking what characteristics are invariably there when one experiences anger or shame or fear or joy as kinds of experiences. The findings of such studies have implications for how we understand ourselves, as well as for psychological practice, because they yield general insights into the "lived meanings" of emotions, perceptions, and problematic behaviors (including their motivational contexts). In the second kind of research, we wish to open up the individual level of experience for a more in-depth understanding, as we might see in case studies where there is a need to grasp the intricacies of human experience.

As a method for embracing both nomothetic and idiographic dimensions of human experience, existential phenomenological research (EPR) draws on both the "pure" phenomenology of Edmund Husserl and the "existential" phenomenological work of Martin Heidegger, Maurice Merleau-Ponty, and Jean-Paul Sartre. On the one hand, Husserl's (1913/1962) "transcendental" philosophical method was aimed toward what he called "universal"

https://doi.org/10.1037/0000257-001
Essentials of Existential Phenomenological Research, by S. D. Churchill

dimensions of consciousness, and this is where his "intuition of essences" can be adapted to produce an understanding of what is most generally true of particular "kinds" of experiences—from the types of emotions felt by all humans to general experiential phenomena such as learning, anxiety, interpersonal attraction, forgiveness, humiliation, gender identity, procrastination, self-esteem, shaming, and victimization, to name a few. On the other hand, there is the possibility of building on Heidegger's (1923/1999, 1927/1962) "existential-hermeneutic" method, which was ultimately aimed toward understanding the individual, particular, and even peculiar ways that people "find themselves" in their everyday world. This aspect of the EPR approach is useful, especially when we are interested in understanding how persons uniquely experience the situations that befall them, as in the case of spinal cord injury, recovery from traumatic injury, or the loss of the other's loving regard. Looking at ordinary experiences through the filters of phenomenological "guiding concepts" (e.g., "intentionality," "in-order-to motives," "existential freedom") and "ways of knowing" (e.g., "empathy," "deep listening," "purifying reflection") can bring rich understanding to a wide range of phenomena. It was Heidegger's (1923/1999) hope that the "existential characteristics" he identified at the most general level could be used to illuminate what is happening in a more nuanced way at the individual level by providing lenses through which to observe and better elucidate what is going on, concepts that "open up" human experience for further inquiry and reflection.

We begin with a sense of curiosity, fascination, and even wonder in the face of some aspect of human experiencing. We hope to gain a better sense of our chosen "phenomenon" through clarification of how it appears to us— that is, through (a) an articulation that enables others to understand what it is we have come to see and understand about the evidence to which we have brought ourselves and (b) the "sense of the whole" that we have developed in bringing ourselves to the encounter with specific kinds of human existence.

This method of research has a 50-year history, beginning with its inception at Duquesne University with the collective work of Colaizzi (1967, 1973, 1978), W. F. Fischer (1974, 1978, 1985), Giorgi (1970, 1975, 1985), Van Kaam (1966), and von Eckartsberg (1971, 1986). Since then, there have been legions of international researchers further developing the methodological work begun at Duquesne (Aanstoos, 1985; Adams, 2016; Angel, 2013; Applebaum, 2014; Ashworth, 2003; Beck, 2021; Churchill, 2000, 2006, 2010b, 2013, 2014, 2016, 2018b; Churchill et al., 1998; Churchill & Wertz, 1985, 2015; Dahlberg et al., 2008; Davidson & Cosgrove, 2003; DeRobertis, 2017; Englander,

2016, 2019, 2020; Finlay, 2011; C. T. Fischer, 1998, 2006; Galvin & Todres, 2013; Garza, 2004, 2007; Gendlin, 1978; Gurwitsch, 1977/1979; Halling, 2008; Halling et al., 2006; Keen, 1975, 2003, 2011, 2012; Kruger, 1979; Langdridge, 2007; Lee, 2016; Morgan, 2011; Morley, 1998, 2010; Morrissey, 2014; Moss, 1982; Moustakas, 1994; Mruk, 2010, 2013; Packer, 2017; Pollio et al., 1998; Romanyshyn, 2007; Smith et al., 2009; Tomkins & Eatough, 2013; Valle, 1998; Valle & Halling, 1989; Van Kaam, 1966, 1987; van Manen, 1990, 2002, 2017; Walsh, 2016; Wertz, 1985, 2010; Wertz et al., 2011).

THE "HUMAN SCIENCE" APPROACH AS A WAY OF SEEING

The heart and soul of the "existential phenomenological" research method is to be found in our "approach" (Giorgi, 1970), which involves how we understand the nature of our subject matter, as well as how we establish our means of access to it. Without this approach—which embodies a distinctive "theory of science" (Dilthey, 1924/1977a; Gurwitsch, 1974, Schütz & Luckmann, 1973)—some of the features of our method might not appear to be different from other qualitative methods. This is because the basic steps of our method are infused from the outset with an understanding of psychological science that is radically different from other researchers, both quantitative and qualitative. The basic theory of science (methodology and epistemology) underlying empirical research methods had remained largely unquestioned during the first century of psychology as a science. The rationale for conducting experiments to determine the "causes" of behavior had been generally taken for granted as the (only) way to do science, notwithstanding a half century of critiques of this paradigm (Churchill, 1991; Gannt & Williams, 2016; Giorgi, 1970, 2009; Koch & Leary, 1985; Strasser, 1963).

Giorgi's (1970) landmark text *Psychology as a Human Science: A Phenomenologically Based Approach* is the seminal work that established the foundations for a qualitative method grounded in the critique of the empirical sciences articulated by Dilthey and Husserl over a century ago. Giorgi introduced the concept of "approach" to clarify the interrelated assumptions underlying scientific practice that has more recently been employed by Levitt et al. (2017), who called on qualitative researchers to connect their research procedures with their philosophical foundations in the name of "methodological integrity." Every aspect of EPR is directly informed by concepts and reflective procedures borrowed directly from phenomenological philosophy. This includes ontological assumptions about what psychological phenomena are and epistemological clarifications regarding how they are best accessed and known.

Most important in my own learning of EPR was acquiring not so much a new "body of information" as a new "way of seeing." This is already informed by the chief insight of phenomenology: namely, that "what you see" (*noema*) is a function of "how you are looking" (*noesis*). This is as true when we are looking at others' behavior as it is when we are looking at movies, paintings, even inkblots. Every "what" is constituted by a particular "how": Every perception is constituted by a unique act of perceiving, every idea by a particular way of understanding. The "how" of our psychological reading of data is informed by a literature that has emerged during the 20th century as a direct consequence of Dilthey's (1924/1977a) famous dictum, "We explain nature; we understand psychological life" (p. 27). To paraphrase: While it is possible to "explain" natural events by means of causal thinking, psychological life requires something else for its elucidation—what the German philosophers called "understanding" (*Verstehen*). When Dilthey (1924/1977a) articulated the foundations of "the human sciences" (*Geisteswissenschaften*) over a century ago, he was naming not just a field of studies, but more important, a particular way of studying that field (see Churchill, 2018a, pp. 70–73, for further clarification of this expression). This field of study aims at elucidating "existential gestalts" or "life as a whole" (Heidegger, 1927/1962, p. 72), beginning with a focus on the individual's point of view. As we shall see, however, the adoption of a phenomenological attitude means much more than simply adopting the other's perspective; it means, rather, the employment of a particular method of reflection on the perspective that is provided to us by our research informants. When we place ourselves as researchers "into" the experiences described to us, we must engage in certain reflective modes of focusing to bring the "phenomena" of human experiencing into view—namely, the acts of human consciousness and their motivational contexts.

As qualitative researchers, we often begin with collecting descriptions from people undergoing the experiences that interest us. The question is, what are we doing when we are reading these descriptions? How are we attending to the words and expressions of our informants? And how do we guard against unwanted biases or preconceptions entering into our findings? Dilthey's (1924/1977a, 1927/1977b) method of understanding was founded on what he called a "sympathy" or "transposition" of oneself into the life context of the person one is attempting to understand. For Dilthey, for us to cultivate a sensitivity to meaning in the lives of others, we must necessarily draw on all the powers of our psyche in observing human experience—not just sensing and judging but feeling, intuiting, imagining, remembering.

The Essential Role of Empathy in EPR

Like Dilthey, Husserl (1952/1989) was interested in our grasping the meaning of others' experience by means of a "pairing" grounded in empathy, whereby we are able to experience the other's perceptions, emotions, cognitions, and volitions through a special kind of access that is mediated by our shared embodiment. Through this "reflexivity" of the body, which enables us to (figuratively speaking) stand on both sides of an encounter simultaneously, we are able to gain access to each other's psychological lives. Husserl (1952/1989) referred to this as "trading places" (p. 177). We do this not only in face-to-face interaction but also when viewing or reading the expressions of the other (including research data). Why is it that I can be moved to tears when I pick up one of my mother's old handwritten letters to me? Is it not because even years later, I am able to still feel her loving presence manifested in the letter itself? Is not the meaning of her words precisely the love that she was so clearly experiencing and revealing in her act of writing? Finally, is not this underlying affection—which constituted my mother's "regard" for me as well as her intention in writing—the ultimate "object" of my perception of her letter?

Other examples of our empathic presence to the other taken from everyday life include when we are dancing with another person and unwittingly mimicking their gestures or when during a movie one's face begins to spontaneously adopt the expressions of the character with whom one is identifying. Film theorists even have a name for this phenomenon: "the scene of empathy" (Plantinga, 1999). A humorous example of this can be found in the film *Play It Again, Sam* (Ross, 1972), which begins with Woody Allen's character sitting spellbound in his seat while watching the ending of *Casablanca* in a movie theater, unconsciously mirroring the facial tics of Humphrey Bogart as he says his goodbyes to Ingrid Bergman in one of the most famous scenes in cinema history. During this scene, Allen is resonating with more than just the facial tics—as he walks out of the theater, he develops a swagger like Bogart. And by the end of the film, we witness him beginning to embody a new *persona*—or what phenomenologists might call a new "intentionality" or way of "being-in-the-world."

The Concept of Intentionality

Once Husserl (1901/1968) had issued forth the "battle cry" of phenomenology—"We want to go back to the 'matters themselves' [*den "Sachen selbst"*] . . . and bring ourselves to the evidence" (p. 6)—it then became a question of determining the nature of the matters that would concern us, as well as the proper mode of access to them. For Husserl (1913/1962, 1925/1977), the phenomena to which we should turn to find evidence for our reflection were the "affairs of consciousness"—which he embraced collectively with the concept of *intentionality*, a term he had derived from Brentano (1874/1973). Even though this term means much more than our deliberate intentions or aims within a situation, the reader can use the idea of there always being some meaning or purpose to be achieved in human behavior (including acts of perceiving, imagining, remembering, feeling, willing, encountering) as a kind of placeholder. In the case of *Play It Again, Sam*, the character's underlying wish was simply to be more like Bogart.

Intentionality is a term that has been used by virtually every phenomenologist and figures prominently in the entire literature of both philosophical and psychological phenomenology. The human, as well as animal, experience of corporeality, spatiality, sociality, and temporality are all subsumed under the rubric of this most important and central philosophical concept of "intentionality." We can say that intentionality refers to the cognitive, perceptual, volitional, emotional, imaginal, and gestural threads that bind us to the world in a meaningful way, albeit in a way that we take for granted. The phenomenological method consists of so many ways to "slacken the intentional threads" (or conscious acts) that connect us to the world, thus bringing them to our attention and making these acts available to reflective analysis (Merleau-Ponty, 1945/1962, p. xiii). This is why phenomenology is often expressed in a language of prepositions (being-*in*, being-*with*, being-*toward*, being-*ahead-of*, *before*-which, *in-order-to*, and so on)—because prepositions describe relationships as seen from a reflective distance, and intentionality is the most generic term we can use to describe the multitude of relationships that define our lives. Van den Berg (1972) distilled all of these into four fundamental relations that he called the relations of oneself to one's world, one's body, other persons, and one's past and future. These relationships, which are accessed through reflective acts of "grasping at meaning," make up what Dilthey (1927/1977b) called "the secret of the person" (p. 177).

Observing and thematizing intentionality became the aim of phenomenologists, as it also became one of the aims of Freud's early "depth psychology." What makes psychoanalysis and phenomenology kindred disciplines is their common interest in the *latent content* revealed in the expressions of psychological life: namely, the "meaning," "motives," and "intentions" of our acts (Freud, 1905/1963, pp. 34, 35, and 37, respectively). It is this "cross validation" of the two fields that led Merleau-Ponty (1960/1969) to famously remark, "Phenomenology and psychoanalysis are not parallel;

much better, they are both aiming toward the same *latency*" (pp. 86–87, italics in original; see also Wertz & Olbert, 2016). What this means for EPR is that what we are attending to is something that does not always lie at the surface of our descriptions but, rather, at their depths. This requires the researcher to try "to get under the data" in the same way that in reading my mother's letters, I was present to more than simply her words. To be present to these depths in a manner that allows us to elucidate them requires the cultivation of a sensitivity to meaning that comes not only from reading primary source literature in phenomenology but also from our life experiences.

Accessing Intentionality

The defining methodological character of EPR is embodied in the illuminating presence of the researcher, who is trained in the use of the phenomenological *epoché*, the phenomenological reduction, some degree of eidetic intuition (the seeing of essences), and use of free variation in the imagination in the move toward generality. I shall briefly define here the first two terms and leave the others to our later chapters.

The Greek term *epoché* refers to a preliminary step whereby the researcher "brackets" or "takes out of play" things that are taken for granted to allow something else to come into view, something we would not be able to see through the distorting lenses of our existing assumptions and beliefs. As Schütz (1962) observed, there are as many *epochai* as there are fields of interest that we may wish to explore because to turn our attention in one direction, we must necessarily turn away from other interests. This is why we employ an *epoché*: To discover an entity or an experience in its own self-givenness, we start by "bracketing" what we have come to know about it. When I take students to the zoo to encounter animal behavior or to a museum to observe human artistic expressions, I ask them to put aside what they think they already know about the species they are about to observe and to bracket the belief that the wheat fields painted by Van Gogh might have "actually" appeared the same way to anyone who was looking over his shoulder. These represent the two primary epochai of the phenomenologist: first, the bracketing of the conceptual prejudices that we carry with us as filters (which can also be "blinders") and, second, the bracketing of the "natural attitude" or belief that the world actually is the way it appears to someone. These two epochai free us to look through the other's eyes without critical judgment, to see and grasp the world as they experience it.

The "phenomenological reduction" is an expression that Husserl (1913/1962) coined, adapted from the Latin *reducere*, which means "to lead" (*ducere*) ourselves "back" (*re-*), or "to restore." For Husserl, this meant, on the one hand, "restoring" the world of perception to see our subject matter as if for the first time, without distorting preconceptions. And on the other hand, it meant "guiding" ourselves "back" from the content of consciousness (which he termed the *noema*) to the conscious act (or *noesis*) that "coconstitutes" that particular content or meaning. The tree standing in the meadow as an "object" of perception may come to have different meanings (*noemata*) for different observers, depending on their particular interests (*noeses*): To the woodsman, the tree might represent fuel for a fire; for two lovers, a place to carve their initials to commemorate their love; for two chipmunks, a place in the branches to construct a habitat. Each perceiver's attitude constitutes a different "meaning" for the tree. To appreciate each act of perceiving the tree, we bracket the question of what the tree (as a self-standing "object") "actually" is. Only then can we bring ourselves back to the "practical" attitude of the woodsman or the "romantic" attitude of the lovers.

This is enough, for now, to introduce some of the basic language of phenomenology. While philosophical phenomenology takes on a wide spectrum of its own research interests, psychological phenomenology leans heavily on the concepts and methods of the existential philosophers, who took phenomenology more in the direction of a science of human persons.

WHAT IS THE KEY INSIGHT OF EXISTENTIAL PHENOMENOLOGY?

Viktor Frankl (1959) put it most simply when he stated that the greatest of human attributes is the freedom "to choose one's attitude in any given set of circumstances" (p. 86). It is precisely this concept of "existential freedom" that is a key insight guiding our research investigations using EPR. In Heidegger's ontology (1927/1962), it was our free (and yet always situated) projection of ourselves into possibilities that defines us. A key to the reading of data by psychologists using EPR can be found in this principle: How does this moment described within the data reveal both the circumstances that situate and (more importantly) the projects that animate this person in this moment of their life?

The "Existential" Approach to the Person

In what is perhaps the most radical statement of 20th-century philosophy, Heidegger (1927/1962) wrote, "The 'essence' of [the human kind] lies in its 'to-be'" (p. 67). He was telling us that what is important is the way that we choose our path (or "to be") in our daily lives, with an interest in our ways of "living" our time—as embodied beings in relation to others and the world. With this statement, Heidegger effectively reoriented our understanding of the "essence" of the human person to be something we can only find in our "to be" (which is future pitched, in contrast to the received view that our essence is to be found in what we already are). In addition, this "to-be" consists of the particular way that each of us "comports ourselves towards our Being" (p. 67). For Heidegger, these aims that we pursue are inextricably bound to how we find ourselves situated. For him, the more important aspect of our "being in the throw" of life is not so much how we find ourselves already thrown as it is our "throwing ourselves forth" into possibilities (pp. 185–186), which he called a "thrown projection." Sartre (1943/1956) then reformulated this with his concept of "situated freedom" (p. 619): It is in the face of our circumstances that we choose how to act (or choose who we shall be).

This philosophy has had a profound influence on how we approach our data as existential phenomenological (EP) researchers. The descriptions we collect tend to be focused more on how participants find themselves "thrown" into their life situations because, when we stop to take note of our circumstances, what stands out most clearly is the observed situation and not our underlying interests and motives within that situation. Our challenge as EP researchers is to discern how, within those circumstances, the participant manages to find possible avenues of choice or meaning making. For the researcher, bringing ourselves back to these acts of meaning making may involve empathy, intuition, and even "reading between the lines" of a description. This discernment may also involve engaging in a dialogue with our informants to seek clarification.

For example, a Japanese American student found herself experiencing social exclusion when she returned home to Japan because she was "excluded" from identifying herself as Japanese by customs officials due to her dual citizenship. For her senior thesis (Watanabe, 2014), this student proposed to study the "effect" of social exclusion on individuals. After being introduced to the literature of EP, she was able to understand better how her social exclusion was a "situation" into which she had been "thrown" by the customs officials and, moreover, that it was up to her to determine whatever "effect" this may or may not have on her. We were thus able to help her reformulate her research question around "how people act in the face of their experiences of social exclusion." These ways of acting are not "effects" that are "caused" by social exclusion; they are rather *choices that one can make in the face of one's circumstances.* We mentored this student by invoking Frankl's (1959) "greatest of human freedoms" and Heidegger's (1927/1962) model of "thrown projection," pointing out how, in the face of exclusion, some people might choose to capitulate to their oppressor, while others may choose to rebel. It is a question of choice. This is what led Sartre (1952/1963) to say, "We are not lumps of clay, and what is important is not what people make of us but what we ourselves make of what they have made of us" (p. 49).

Existential Choice and Transcendence

Rejecting the idea that we can reduce our behaviors to being a simple function of environmental and bodily variables as one finds in some forms of experimental psychology, Sartre's (1943/1956) "existential psychoanalysis" took its cue from Heidegger in recognizing that the way human persons live their lives is always, implicitly, according to some orientation toward the future. Whereas, in experimental psychology, the present psychological state is presumed to be "caused" by the immediate conditions within which it has occurred, for Sartre, the actual "sequence" is the opposite. Our future-pitched goals in the present moment create for us the meaning of our situation, within which we are challenged to find our bearings. Even going out on a weekend evening for a soiree can be rife with anticipations, fantasies, expectations, desires that are all a function of choices we make without even noticing. Human freedom consists of our freedom to transcend the circumstances in which we find ourselves: It is by choice that we move forward within our circumstances. It is important to remember that our choices are not always deliberate intentions: "When I deliberate, the chips are down" (Sartre, 1943/1956, p. 581). Thus, intentionality can be revealed in spontaneous acts, as well as acts that might be premeditated. "Any way you look at it, it is a matter of choice" (p. 708).

For example, even our emotions, typically understood as passive states that we "suffer," express a latent intentionality: Anger can sometimes be reframed as a way of transcending our having been hurt by someone who now appears to us as hateful. In a similar fashion, if we find ourselves fearful of a group of people, we might choose to vilify them. Sartre's analysis shows how this "new" quality of the other (as hateful) is not a simple given but, rather, my meaningful ("intentional") way of transforming the other into someone stripped of the power to hurt me. This "hateful" trait now "seen" in the other (which in self-deception I experience as a simple fact) is actually the correlate of a "choice" made by myself—a choice that can be shown to have a purpose, a meaning. My anger is thus not a simple "response" like a reflex; rather, it is a "preemptory strike" against the power of the other to affect me (C. T. Fischer, 1998; see also Sartre, 1939/1948, p. 91).

In a simple example drawn from everyday life, let us consider the mother who confronts her son for hitting his little brother, asking him, "Why did you do that?" The little boy responds, "Because I hate him!" "And why do you hate your brother?" asks the mother, to which the boy replies, "Because he makes me so mad!" And then, as if to further justify his action, the boy adds, "I hit him because he hit me first!" Either way, he is appealing to a "because-motive" or "reason" for his behavior, one that seems to get him off the hook. His mother might then respond, "But is this the kind of boy that you want to grow up to be, the one who hurts his little brother?" An existential approach might teach us to grasp that in hitting his little brother back, the boy was realizing himself as "the one who does not suffer indignities" and that it was his "choice of being" that ultimately led him to identify his having been hit first by his little brother as the reason for his response. The phenomenological reduction, when practiced by the existential psychologist, leads us back to the "choices of being" that underlie our behavior.

Note that in this example, the little boy could have expressed a more proximate intention as the "reason" for his hitting his brother: "to get even" with him. EPR is less concerned with such obvious or "proximate" aims as it is with the more overarching but less obvious ones. "Why did you hit your brother?" is a question that can be answered superficially with reference to either "because" or "in-order-to" motives. EPR is, however, going more for the deeper meanings, the more latent (less obvious) intentionalities that faithfully reveal what is at work in our experience. And this is indeed a part of EPR's "methodological fidelity" to its subject matter—namely, human intentionality.

Circular Temporality Versus Linear Determinism

Unlike the events studied by the natural sciences that follow a linear "cause-and-effect" model of temporality within its "theory of science" (one that yields explanations), the events of human psychological life follow a profoundly different temporality, as seen from within the theory of science of EPR. If anything, there is a "circular causality" by means of which my projection of a self that I want to be constitutes the basis for my choices in the present moment, which then take up and transform my immediate situation or my "past." It was my purpose to preserve my sense of myself as having value that motivated me to see the other—who a moment ago hurt my feelings—as hateful. The alarm that rings in the morning is not the "reason" that I get out of bed to start my day; if the alarm has any significance, it is the meaning that it has for my "project-to-be"—in this case, to be the kind of person who gets to work on time. Thus, to get up at the sound of the alarm is to realize the possibility of becoming this self that I choose to be. This would be the structure of all our "agentive" actions. Furthermore, we are responsible for all our actions; there are no excuses. Do I stay off the grass in the public park "because" of the sign that says "Keep off the Grass"? Or does the sign, like the alarm that rings in the morning, only have the weight that my free project and the self to be realized confers on it? It is in our "not yet"—rather than in what "already exists"—that we shall truly find ourselves. In this sense, where one is going determines "the meaning" of where one has been.

A simple thought experiment illustrates this: When we look retrospectively at our life, we tend to see where we are now as a function of the various ways our past has "led" us to where we are today. It almost seems as though there was a "linear determinism" at work, where time flows in a linear fashion from past to present to future. Perhaps this is what makes psychological theories so appealing to us: They seem to "explain" how we got to where we are. But what if you were to have chosen to attend a different college or take up a different major? You would look back on the same past to justify how you ended up in this alternate universe. But would it really be the "same past" anymore? Or would it be the past as seen anew—from the point of view of your new goals, the very goals that led you to choose a different college or a different major? We see at once that the "meaning" of various aspects of our past only has the weight that my free "choice of being" confers on it. If I choose to one day be a doctor, then when I look back on my past, I see all the "reasons why" I ended up where I am: I selectively attend to my past experiences, which stand out now against the backdrop of my choice to realize myself as a physician. What I "see" when I reflect back on my past are all of the obvious "reasons" that "made me" what I am today. The self that I am is a function of the self that I project myself to be, and the meaning of my past is retrofit to the contours of my imagined future. This is the meaning of "existential temporality."

This circularity in our relation to time also carries over into our relationships with the world in general, including our social relations. Heidegger (1924/2011) established that *signification*—which he called "the world's primary ontological characteristic"—is revealed in "the [particular] way in which we encounter the surrounding world" (p. 17). He further clarified that the meanings of the world that are signified to us in daily life are the function of a relational "in order to" that expresses our "concerned engagement with the world" (p. 17). Because these significations and their constitution are among the primary aims of data analysis in EPR, an understanding of the modes of reflection by which we can access them is of great importance to us.

"In-Order-to Motives" Versus "Because Motives"

Sartre (1943/1956, pp. 211–237) distinguished between two ways of knowing in his characterization of "impure reflection" (*explanation*) as the method of reflection that gives us linear determinism and "purifying reflection" (*understanding*) as giving us existential temporality. The linear determinism constituted by "impure reflection" gives us what Schütz (1932/1967, 1970) simply called the "because motives" for our current actions, while the future-oriented temporality given to us in Sartre's purifying reflection reveals what Schütz referred to collectively as our "in-order-to motives." By definition, "the in-order-to motive refers to the attitude of the actor living in the process of his ongoing action" (Schütz, 1970, p. 128).

> To him [the actor], motive means what he has actually in view as bestowing meaning upon his ongoing action, and this is always the in-order-to-motive, the intention to bring about a projected state of affairs, to attain a pre-conceived goal. As long as the actor lives in his ongoing action, he does not have in view its because motives. . . . In using the linguistic form "in-order-to," I am looking at the ongoing process of action which is still in the making and appears therefore in the time perspective of the future. (Schütz, 1970, pp. 127–128)

The problem comes when people are asked to look back and reflect, because then they are no longer "living in their ongoing action." This can tend to put the average person into the position of identifying "because" motives, which they tend to do imperfectly (when looking in the time perspective of the past). This led one colleague to develop a "think-aloud method" for capturing the ongoing thought process of chess players in action (Aanstoos, 1985). (This is something to keep in mind when we are collecting descriptions of lived experiences "after the fact." We end up having to "see through" the erroneous accounts—as we shall later discover—to regain "the time perspective of the future.") As we see in Chapter 4, it is indeed my task as researcher to place myself in the position of the person describing their experience in an effort to vicariously become "the actor living in the process of their ongoing action" and thereby to gain a glimpse into possible in-order-to motives for that action. This "viewing" of the other's motivational horizons was described by Husserl as a specific kind of seeing that is grounded in empathy (Husserl, 2006, pp. 84–86; see also Churchill, 2016, p. 102, and 2018a).

Sartre (1939/1948) observed that it requires a special "existential" interest in human behavior to reveal our true in-order-to motives. More typically, we engage in the kind of "impure" reflection that attempts to identify the reasons "because of which" we have acted in a particular way. For Sartre, it is actually self-deceptive for us to believe that our behavior is explainable in the same way that we explain nonhuman things—that is, in terms of reasons and causes. Certainly, there are entities that passively submit to the forces of nature, in which case we "explain" them as following linear sequences of cause and effect. Whereas, in our approach to human beings, we need a new way of thinking—one that can open up for our understanding the field of human relationality—"purified" of all explanations.

If "impure reflection" gives us a conception of time that assigns the meaning of our acts to antecedent causes, it is through a "purifying reflection" that we are able to establish the foundation for human action in our freely chosen "projects" or goals (Sartre, 1952/1963, pp. 91ff, 150ff). Many psychological "explanations" of behavior have served this human tendency toward impure reflection whereby we strive to find reasons and causes for our acts rather than genuinely "owning" them. Sartre (1943/1956) observed,

> Psychological determinism, before being a theoretical conception, is first an attitude of excuse, or if you prefer, the basis of all attitudes of excuse. . . . it asserts that there are within us antagonistic forces whose type of existence is comparable to that of things. It attempts to fill the void [of uncertainty] which encircles us, to re-establish the links between past and present, between present and future. (p. 40)

As we have seen, in the "impure reflection" that constitutes "because motives," the immediate past produces the present moment: In our earlier example, my present feeling of anger is assumed to be "caused" by the entrance of a hateful person in the scene. For Sartre, the actual "sequence" is the opposite: Present intentions bearing on the immediate future produce the meaning of the past as a context or "situation." As we have seen in our earlier examples, the "self that awaits me in the future" motivates my present acts rather than the other way around. This will extend to how (in Chapter 4) we "approach" our work as researchers in trying to "understand" rather than "explain" what is going on in our data, with an ultimate goal of revealing our participants' life choices. It is the attitude of "purifying reflection" that relieves us from thinking in terms of linear determinism by placing ourselves imaginatively back into the other's "ongoing process of

FIGURE 1.1. Purifying Reflection Versus Impure Reflection

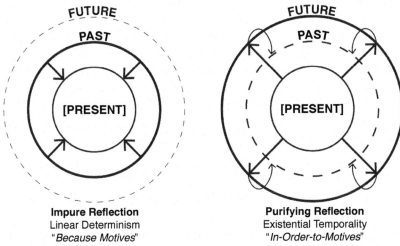

Impure Reflection	Purifying Reflection
Linear Determinism	Existential Temporality
"Because Motives"	*"In-Order-to-Motives"*

Note. Linear determinism is shown here to be a consequence of an "impure reflection" that points to "because motives" to "explain" behavior–through an appeal to antecedent events taken as "causes." Behavior is viewed as a "response" (like a reflex) rather than as an "act" (implying an actor or agent), and the future has no explanatory weight. Purifying reflection, which is Sartre's (1943/1956) version of the phenomenological reduction (with its bracketing of reductionistic explanations), brings us face to face with our "in-order-to" motives, revealing a future-oriented temporality where we "understand" the self that awaits me in the future as the motivation for my present (and past) acts.

action, which is still in the making" to make "the time perspective of the future" appear. For impure reflection, the future hardly exists; for purifying reflection, our relationship to our immediate future embodies the direction of our intentionality. Figure 1.1 is an attempt to illustrate this contrast between the principle of *causality* inherent in impure reflection and the principle of *intentionality* inherent in purifying reflection.

SUMMARY

You can begin to see now how all this "philosophy" finds its way into our research method. Purifying reflection establishes our grasp of freedom, revealing our acts as motivated, not simply by "because" motives but, more important, by "in-order-to" motives—not by "the past" but by "the self that awaits me in the future." When reflecting on the experiences of others, "we imaginatively project the in-order-to motive of the other person as if it were our own and then use the fancied carrying-out of such an action as a scheme in which to [grasp at the meaning of] his lived experiences" (Schütz, 1970, p. 177). Ultimately, with EPR, you will be looking not for the effects of circumstances on people but, rather, for the choices we make in the face of our circumstances. In our free choice to realize ourselves in one way or another, we discover the meaning, the significance, the underlying "intent" of our actions. EPR is a method that enables us to attend to the meaning and motivational contexts of these choices.

In Exhibit 1.1, I summarize the characteristics that make this method at once scientific, phenomenological, and existential.

EXHIBIT 1.1. Key Features of Existential Phenomenological Research

The following are key features of the existential phenomenological research (EPR) method:

- The method is a rigorously "scientific" research method because it is evidence based.

- The nature of the evidence is the description of the "affairs of our psychological life."

- These affairs are the conscious acts (the "matters themselves") to which we return in "bringing ourselves to the evidence" (Husserl, 1901/1968, p. 6).

- The method is "phenomenological" not just because we begin with first-person descriptions of experience (after all, this is true of most qualitative research) but primarily because the researcher's *method of reflection* on those experiences follows methodologically prescribed procedures borrowed from phenomenology, including
  - *epoché* (bracketing preconceptions, suspending belief),
  - *intuition* (encountering or "looking at" something),
  - *reduction* (a manner of focusing, "leading oneself back" to meanings),
  - *intentional analysis* (seeing and thematizing individual moments within a whole),
  - *imaginative variation* (to arrive at what is essential), and
  - *synthesis* (to see and articulate how the moments within an experience function together within the "whole" of that experience).

- The method is "existential" because it focuses on experiences as they manifest themselves within the flow of human existence, defined in terms of how we transcend our circumstances toward possibilities of our own choosing.

The key features of the EPR theory of science:

- The phenomenological principle of intentionality is favored over the explanatory principle of causality.

- Existential choice and transcendence are the focus rather than reductive assertions of cause-and-effect.

- EPR approaches human temporality as fundamentally distinct from the non-telic temporality of natural phenomena: We find that "in-order-to" motives are more important than "because" motives in assessing the meaning of human experience.

EXHIBIT 1.1. Key Features of Existential Phenomenological Research
(*Continued*)

- "Because" motives tend to be self-deceptive; one encounters them frequently in naive descriptions of experience: "I am angry because he is hateful."

- "In-order-to" motives are more genuinely revealing of human meaning: "I unwittingly experience him as hateful in order to escape from the hurt I was feeling a moment ago."

- The "how" of EPR: The researcher engages in existential contact with the phenomenon under investigation, whether through direct or vicarious experience. To access meaningful experiences through participants' descriptions requires that the researcher cultivate a sensitivity to meaning as well as a strongly developed sense of empathy.

- The "whence and the whither" of EPR: We begin with a sense of curiosity, fascination, even wonder in the face of some aspect of human experiencing. We hope to gain a better sense of our chosen "phenomenon" through clarification of how it appears to us and an articulation that enables others to grasp what we have come to see and understand about the evidence to which we have brought ourselves.

2 GETTING STARTED

Selecting an Experience to Study

One of the nice things about being a phenomenological researcher is that just about any experience can be a topic of interest. The tricky part comes in focusing on some aspect of the experience to study so that we can find within these experienced situations something that we can call "meaning making" on the part of our research participants. In one sense, doing psychology phenomenologically can be described as a process of starting with the meanings found within descriptions of situations lived through by our informants and working our way back to the latent intentionalities that "made" those circumstances what they were for the participant. Although just about any "lived experience" can be the subject matter for analysis, the method of existential phenomenological research (EPR) is well suited for studying situations in which people have something at stake, something with which they are "coming to terms." When people find themselves in circumstances where they must make a choice or when they are living through emotional situations where they have lost their bearings, these experiences are well suited for analysis using EPR.

In this chapter, we go over the process of (a) formulating a research question, sometimes called a "research interest"; (b) formulating "access

https://doi.org/10.1037/0000257-002
Essentials of Existential Phenomenological Research, by S. D. Churchill

questions" to pose to participants to get them started thinking about their experience while prompting them to write a description or a story that will serve as data; and (c) engaging in follow-up interviews for clarification of the data. Along the way, we shall distinguish the research phenomenon from the lived experiences that reveal it to help the reader understand how psychological phenomena are embedded within situations and require a sensitivity to meaning to bring them to the surface.

FORMULATING A RESEARCH QUESTION

Ideally, following Heidegger's analysis of the threefold structure of "asking a question" (*fragen*), one would begin with (a) a sense of what is asked for— a clarification of a concept or an understanding of some aspect of psychological life that will better enable therapists to work with their clients (the list would be endless)—but whatever is "asked for" (the *Erfragte*), there is (b) a corresponding research phenomenon that is then "asked about" (the *Gefragte*), and (c) a situation or lived experience that is then "being asked" or interrogated (the *Befragte*) to bring the "asked about" to light (Heidegger, 1985, pp. 144–146; 1927/1962, p. 24). In psychological research, these three aspects correspond to the *research question* or "purpose" of inquiry (*Gefragte*), the *data* or "object" of inquiry (*Befragte*), and the *findings* or "outcome" of inquiry (*Erfragte*). In the case of phenomenologically based qualitative research, the researcher is faced with the task of finding a situation that will serve as an adequate and accessible location or vehicle for the appearance of the research phenomenon. The research can thus be described as an investigation "of" the situation selected for study, "about" the phenomenon of interest to the researcher (Churchill, 2018b). The research thus (ideally) proceeds with a clear sense of the research question from the outset; this, then, informs the literature review, as well as the targeting of experiences to be studied qualitatively.

For example, one of our recent students had been influenced by her reading of de Beauvoir and Sartre in relation to the psychological impact of "the other's regard" and especially by an earlier thesis devoted to "experiencing oneself as being beautiful" (Rao & Churchill, 2004). She became interested in studying the conflict between the feeling we have of ourselves from the inside and how we are perceived by others. How is our intentionality with regard to "being seen by the other" revealing of our sense of self, our need to manage others' impressions of us, and our emotions and frustrations in the face of feeling misrecognized by the other's regard? These kinds of interests made up our student's "research questions"—that is, the questions to be posed while examining the data. However, to obtain data to use in this study, the student had to select a particular situation that could reveal such dimensions of the female experience (because she was particularly interested in women's experience of themselves in relation to the other), and then she had to come up with a "prompt" to get her participants talking about this experience. The prompt or "access question" that she posed to her participants was,

> Describe a situation in which you were seen without makeup, when you were specifically not expecting to be seen in that way. Describe the situation fully like a story with a beginning, middle, and end; paying particular attention to your focus on being seen by the other. (Tenreiro, 2017, p. 17)

Her research was not about makeup, nor was it about "person perception" or "interpersonal attraction" as traditionally defined by social psychologists. She was careful to only allude to intentionality (through reference to the participant's "not expecting to be seen in that way") without explicitly placing the focus for the participant on her intentionality. The participants were asked to focus not on their interior life but on the situation, which for them became a problematic one. In directing the participant's focus to the situation of "being seen without makeup," the researcher's intention was to provide a safe context within which the participant might reveal otherwise unexpressed meanings pertaining to how she wishes to be perceived. These dimensions would include her implicit "project" to be perceived in a particular way, as well as how she is affected by the intersection of that project and the other's regard. Notice that the access question posed as a prompt to the participant points directly to the situation and only indirectly to the phenomenon—even though this phenomenon of living in the eyes of others was the "real" research interest. The situation selected for study and the question posed to the participant were both intended to give the researcher access to the phenomenon that lies buried, waiting to be revealed.

Distinguishing Research Interests From Access Questions

Hopefully, the reader can see from the example that the access question (that is, the question posed to the participant) is nothing more than a stimulus to get the participant to write about their experience. The question itself can be straightforward, such as "Please describe an emotional experience," or it can be more complex, such as the access question quoted earlier. The questions that we keep in the back of our minds as we read the data are the "research interests" that will guide the analysis. However, we do not always want to pose those questions to our informants. EPR is more of an exploratory method; that is, we are not seeking to confirm hypotheses. The questions that we use as prompts for our participants need to be posed in such a way as to evoke descriptions without telling them too much about what (we think) we are looking for. These "access questions" are typically formulated more as a way of inviting the participant to open up—with the hope of their preparing an elaborated description of some lived-through situation that we believe we can use to apprehend the phenomenon of interest.

Indirect Questioning

Sometimes, for reasons of sensitivity to the feelings of our human participants, we do not ask our questions directly. Psychologists might be interested in how events such as spinal cord injury, cancer surgeries (breast, vaginal, prostate, testicular, and so on), or simple aging can affect changes in people's ability to engage in intercourse. The phenomenon might be tentatively characterized as "sexual dysphoria following surgery," and the research question might ultimately be "How does this surgery affect both the ability of the patient to engage with intimate others and to feel pleasure during the process?" To ask the question in that manner, however, already gives the impression that the researcher might be expecting the effect of the surgery to be negative. An access question needs to be more neutral with regard to whether the impact of the surgery is positive or negative. And certainly, in terms of the ethics of research with human participants, we do not wish to make someone now realize that there is even more for them to feel regretful about than before the research started. A more sensitive access question might begin by saying, "Let's move into some of the ways that your surgery has come to play in your social relationships. In particular, I would like to ask you to talk about your romantic life." An indirect and open-ended "question" such as this does not suggest that their romantic relationships have been affected in any bad way; even the use of the word "play" casts a more positive, encouraging light on the possibilities opened up (as well as closed off) by the surgery. Indeed, for some individuals, an impediment to engaging in intercourse might come as a welcome relief to what had become a drudgery to them while opening up new avenues for exploring their relationships with intimate others.

Open-Ended Research Interests

Access questions that do not point beyond the targeted situation selected for study to a more defined research interest can occur when there is a lack of focus, such as in exploratory research. The reality is that the ability to hold onto a research interest while posing an access question that cleverly points "elsewhere" (as we saw in the case of the study of "being seen without makeup") is not always the case, especially in first-time research projects. Student research studies are, for the most part, "works in progress," especially when you are engaging in pilot research or exploratory research where you are searching for a phenomenon to investigate. In those cases, you will find that there is less clarity with regard to your research question at the outset, and you will end up "finding your way" to your phenomenon. I have found that qualitative data-based phenomenological research often begins with the researcher first identifying an experience or a situation that they are interested in studying, without any apparent reason. Sometimes, it seems as though identifying an experience to interrogate has taken the place of identifying a research question.

For example, one student wanted to ask his participants to describe their experience of engaging in competitive sports. When asked what he wanted to discover about this experience as a student of psychology, he replied, "I just want to follow the data and see where it leads." When asked whether he had any ideas about where this study might lead him, the student was not sure. This same thing has happened countless times with students entering our qualitative research seminars with a "situation" or "lived experience" to be studied without a guiding question in regard to what psychological phenomenon is being pursued. (For further examples of studies where the researchers got "lost in the trees" because they did not proceed with a clear enough "sense of the forest," see Churchill, 1990, pp. 54–55; 2018b, pp. 217–219.)

The point is that once you have selected a realm of human experience for study (Heidegger's *Befragte*), you still face the challenge of deciding on what it is you wish to find out about this experience (the *Gefragte*). This is part of what Moustakas (1990) referred to as the "heuristic" dimension of qualitative research–namely, the student's "finding their way" to a topic. The task of coming up with a clear research question can itself be one of the greatest challenges facing the researcher; in fact, it is often the case that students—even at the doctoral level—do not fully grasp the question they are posing until well after the research is in progress. This means that I encourage you, especially if you are just starting out with EPR, to engage in a certain amount of piloting, to test the waters, so to speak, and see what kinds of themes emerge in descriptions of lived experiences, especially because in your first efforts, you are likely to select your "situation to be described" before identifying the underlying psychological "phenomenon" that you will be investigating.

Distinguishing the Research Phenomenon From the Situation That Reveals It

As we have seen, an access question asks about a situation that has been lived through and tries to point the participant in a particular direction within that situation. In the example given earlier, the lived experience taken as the "object" of inquiry (the *Befragte*) was "a situation in which you were seen without makeup, when you were specifically not expecting to be seen in that way." The research interest (the *Gefragte*), as the reader may recall, was not about wearing or not wearing makeup. It was about the experience of being seen by the other and how in such experiences, "being seen by the other is an occasion for the female's 'self' to be questioned and even put at risk" (Tenreiro, 2017, p. 15). It was indeed to address this research interest as the "purpose" of the inquiry (the *Gefragte*) that the access question was carefully formulated to include the directive for the participants to pay "particular attention to your focus on being seen by the other" (Tenreiro, 2017, p. 17). The researcher here was informed by de Beauvoir (1949/2010), who had suggested that "the gaze is danger" (p. 294), insofar as the girl's sense of self-worth derives less typically from her actions than from the praise of others (p. 372, cited by Tenreiro, 2017, p. 15).

Psychological Phenomena Revealed as Embedded Within Life Situations

To teach someone how to raise a genuine "research question" (which is the same thing as helping them to discover their "research interest"), it is essential that the researcher already has come to appreciate the difference between a psychological "phenomenon" (as defined phenomenologically) and the "situation" or "lived experience" or "life circumstances" within which that psychological phenomenon is embedded. Sartre (1939/1948) defined phenomenological psychology as the study of "people *in situations*" (p. 19, italics in original). "Situation is a good construct . . . because it can contain all the particular strands of activities and experiences as they may happen and as they are given to the experience of the individual on multiple levels" (von Eckartsberg, 1971, p. 76). What a researcher wishes to study within any particular situation would then be something that "shows itself" or "appears" to the researcher from within that situation; "that which shows itself to an observer" is an abbreviated definition of the term *phenomenon*. The tricky part is when we are talking about psychological phenomena that often only show themselves indirectly within life circumstances. A good fisherman has to "know" where to cast their line. Lakes and rivers are "situations" or "circumstances" in which one can find fish. The fish, like research phenomena, often remain hidden within the bodies of water (or "situations") that contain them. So, fishing requires that we (a) know what kinds of fish we are after and (b) know where to look for them. In phenomenological research, the meanings that we are seeking are "context dependent" (Englander, 2019), and this means that we need to think about what contexts (situations, life experiences) we can select that will reveal our sought-after meanings.

In EPR, we can begin by drawing a distinction between the experience that is to be described and the latent meanings or significations within that situation that the investigation aims to bring to light. For example, in a study of test anxiety, the "situation" can be described as "that in the face of which" the person experiences anxiety—the particular test they were taking that made them anxious. The "meanings" of the anxious situation would be the "aim" of the study—namely, to disclose the "significations" of the psychological phenomenon of anxiety, such as "what will become of me if I fail to do well on this test?" These signified meanings can be described as "that about which" one is conducting the investigation; we shall refer to it here as the "research phenomenon," to which we will ultimately address our formal research questions—namely, what is at stake for the anxious student? Who will they be (or fail to become) if they do not pass this exam? Our research questions must help us approach (a) the places where we find our phenomena (the *Befragte*, or situations interrogated), (b) the phenomena "looked for" in those places (the *Gefragte*), and (c) the psychological meanings to be discovered (the *Erfragte*).

Making this kind of distinction between the situation and the phenomenon is analogous to the traditional distinction between stimulus and response, except for one big difference: In EPR, the response is not just an automatic reflex but rather a choice. And it is these choices that make up our research phenomena. Learning to appreciate the distinction between the circumstances that affect us and the choices we can make within those circumstances is the first lesson of EPR.

Coming to Terms With One's Life Circumstances

One of our recent research students (Miranda, 2016) wanted to study the experience of miscarriage. She collected data from her mother and aunts, who had experienced miscarriages, and presented her data in class. One of the things I noticed was that in her analysis of the data, she would say, for example, "The participant lamented that her womb was a graveyard" or "The participant was happy that her mission on earth is fulfilled because she has been sending babies to Jesus." There were other statements like this in her "first impressions" of the data, and I had written at the top of her class handout, "Coming to terms with miscarriage." When she was finished presenting, I commented to the class how her data were a good example of what Heidegger (1923/1999) meant when he talked about how each person, in facing up to their circumstances, is involved in a struggle to make sense of their experience.

There is always a self-interpretation going on when anyone tries to understand what they are going through. And essentially, we as researchers are tapping into that process when we engage in collecting descriptions of experiences from our informants. In this sense, early developers of EPR sometimes referred to our research participants as "coresearchers" (von Eckartsberg, 1971). In this case, the student's analysis revealed to me that she was not studying "miscarriage" per se; she was rather studying each of her participants' "coming to terms" with their miscarriages. The "experience of miscarriage" was the situation studied; the informants' acts of meaning making in "coming to terms" with miscarriage constituted the phenomenon elucidated by the research. Once we had clarified this for the student, the research question that emerged from the student's pilot study was, "How did these women 'come to terms with' their miscarriages?" The whole point is to emphasize how the research question aims at a phenomenon that lies within a lived situation.

What We Are "Looking At" Versus What We Are "Looking For"

In our way of characterizing human science research, a research investigation can be seen as a study "of" someone's experience "about" the lived meanings inherent in that experience. The situation provides a focus, something to be "looked at," whereas the true subject matter of study—what we are "looking for"—would be the latent "intentionality" or meaning-making acts of the participant that are awaiting discovery and explication. Giorgi (2009) sometimes referred to the research process as one of *explicitation*, in the sense of making explicit what was originally implicit in experience as it was lived (pp. 81–82).

A few more examples will hopefully make this distinction clear, beginning with my attempt at conducting a phenomenological study for my doctoral dissertation. I was initially interested in understanding what makes a psychologist's way of seeing distinctive from other kinds of seeing. My first challenge was to identify a "vehicle" for my study: a situation to be interrogated that would reveal the psychological attitude at work. I eventually settled on the psychodiagnostic interview as what I decided to call my "research situation"—a designation that had not been used in dissertations to date;

so, this represented an innovation in design that unfortunately was not yet grasped by those who were guiding me. Oddly, as soon as I selected this situation to reveal the psychological attitude, two of my research advisors began telling me that my "phenomenon" was now the assessment interview itself and that my research question to be posed to the data would be "How does an assessment happen?" After a year of working under this guidance, the title of my research proposal ended up naming just the situation to be studied (what the research would be "a study of")—namely, "The Interview Phase of Diagnostic Assessment as Lived by the Clinical Psychologist." It was not until I had spent almost 2 years lost in the data that I realized, with the help of my third advisor, that I had lost sight of my original research interest, which had more to do with how a psychologist is experientially present during the clinical interview such that something psychological is revealed about the patient. "Clinical intuition" or "psychodiagnostic seeing" turned out to be a better descriptor of my phenomenon, and I eventually found my way back on track. In my dissertation, I included a clarification of this phenomenon versus situation distinction in my "methodological contributions" (Churchill, 1984, pp. 193–196, 210).

To recap: From my experience of having gotten lost in the trees, I came to realize that it is important that student researchers attempting to employ phenomenology learn to ask, "What is the person's latent intentionality (meanings, motives, intentions) within this experience that has been described?" Here, the term *intentionality* points to the meaning-making acts on the part of the participant during the experienced situation described in their data. By *latent*, I mean to acknowledge that in people's descriptions of their lived experiences, the intentionality is quite often "implicit" or only "alluded to" in the original descriptions. The purpose of the follow-up interview is indeed to try to "flush out" these intentions, motives, and aims that presumably lie at the root of the behaviors and experiences described—and that, in turn, are "signified" by the description. Indeed, it is the phenomenological "reduction" that "leads us back" to these meanings from our starting point in the data.

As another example, a few years ago, my senior thesis coteacher and I inherited a class of students, a good number of whom had recently taken a class in experimental design and had written their research proposals asking what the effect was of some set of circumstances on the person who experiences them: the effect of the death of a child on the parents, the effect of parental divorce on their children, the impact of a "special needs" child born into a family, and so on. My colleague and I were faced with the challenge of helping these students to see that their point of entry into the study of each of these circumstances would be not to look for the direct "effect" of those circumstances on the persons describing them but rather to ask what the coconstituted "meaning" was of these circumstances for the individuals who underwent them and how they charted their course through these circumstances. For example, the "special needs" child became recast in the final analysis as bearing the meaning of a "gift" to the family. What we were doing was reframing their research questions from the experimental approach—where the students appeared to be seeking the "effect" of an independent variable (which in each case was some set of circumstances thrust on the individual)—to a more existential approach in which those circumstances were viewed as a starting point from which the individual had a number of options and, in the end, found a way of choosing their possibilities in their own particular way. The research questions were thus effectively reframed from looking for a general "effect" to looking for individual "choices."

In one final example, a student interested in studying women who have remained in abusive relationships began by thinking of her topic in terms of the phenomenon of "learned helplessness." As we reviewed her proposal in class, it occurred to me that learned helplessness was an explanatory construct that served to account for how a state of helplessness occurred over time. That is, it appeals to the trappings of learning theory to suggest to us that earlier situations from which the person had sought escape were inescapable; the escape behavior proved inefficacious, and thus the behavior became extinct. This construct may help us as psychologists to explain how this experience might have come about, but it does not do us much good in the way of helping us to understand a particular individual's pattern of helplessness.

A phenomenological paradigm would not seek explanation but rather understanding: To understand domestic abuse is not to explain how one learns to be helpless but rather to become more acutely aware of the psychological conditions that make possible a helpless stance rather than a proactive one. What would the phenomenologically oriented researcher be looking for in self-report data describing an abused woman's situation? I think it would be something along the lines of the person's way of "being in" the situation such that there seems to be no way out. The woman perceives her situation as inescapable; this meaning (what Husserl called the *noema*) is the intentional correlate of a particular way of being present to her possibilities (what Husserl called *noesis* or "intending act"). Following Husserl's (1913/1962) method of intentional analysis as adapted here, we might ask, "What is it about her mode of presence that disempowers her?" Here, we look to the facts of her situation not for an explanation of her helplessness but for a point of entry into her way of perceiving her possibilities within her social world. How does she continue to live in this dysfunctional conjugal situation? How does she coconstitute her relationships to others such that she does not experience herself as empowered to reject and free herself from abusive situations?

In a more recent study of the same phenomenon, I guided my advisee to follow what Heidegger (1927/1962) referred to as Dilthey's "psychological hermeneutics" (p. 450), which refers to the human being's effort to understand their circumstances (Churchill, 2013; Heidegger, 1923/1999). If the way we "project" ourselves into life situations is always a function of how we have managed to interpret the meaning of our circumstances, then a woman's choice to actually leave a situation of abuse may turn out to be a function of how she understands the particular circumstances in which she "finds herself"—specifically, whether she is able to imagine viable alternatives. The question, then, became how the research participants were able to find their way out of these circumstances, as opposed to always managing to find their way back to the relationships of abuse (Gosline, 2016).

SUMMARY

In this chapter, we have prepared the novice to anticipate and hopefully resolve any confusion between the psychological phenomenon of interest and the situations selected to manifest the phenomenon. The ultimate aim of EPR is to develop a structural understanding of a psychological phenomenon at individual (situated) levels of analysis, as well as a more general (trans-situational) level. I have tried to demonstrate how easy it can be to "lose sight of" one's research phenomenon when one is too focused on the "lived experience" within which the research interest is embedded. The aim of the phenomenological reduction is to lead ourselves back from the situation (or lived experience) directly interrogated (Heidegger's *Befragte*) to the phenomenon "about which" we are ultimately interested (the *Gefragte*). Once the researcher has clarified this distinction as it pertains to their research, they are ready to begin collecting data.

3

COLLECTING THE DATA

Variations exist in how existential phenomenological (EP) researchers have formulated their research questions and collected data from their participants. In this chapter, I offer a schematic outline of the recommended process, along with a discussion of how each of these steps of the overall research process takes its distinctive nature from the philosophical considerations presented in the earlier chapters. But first, I turn to some preliminary ethical considerations.

ATTENDING TO ETHICAL CONSIDERATIONS

In the conduct of human science research, it is always important to be mindful of how powerful the experience of being questioned about one's experience can be to a participant. Class exercises aside, when we begin to collect data from informants, we need to think about whether the questions we pose to them might make them anxious, sad, or even despondent. I was discussing this issue with a nursing colleague who wanted to ask her spinal cord–injured patients about various aspects of their experience of being

https://doi.org/10.1037/0000257-003
Essentials of Existential Phenomenological Research, by S. D. Churchill

paraplegic. We discussed how difficult it might be to ask them to speak about what might be unspeakable for them, such as how their injury has affected their sexuality, love life, and capability for conjugal relations.

Concern for Human Participants

Whenever engaging in a method of research that is likely to penetrate to deeper layers of experience, including those that people tend to keep hidden from others, we need to be mindful and facilitative of the well-being of our participants. In some research seminars, it is not unusual for practice interviews involving class participants to surprise our student-participant when they find themselves holding back tears in response to questions that come up, often quite innocently, from their classmates. For this reason, we often have the student whose data we are analyzing in class leave the room so that the rest of the students can discuss, under supervision, how to ask questions that are not "leading" and, at the same time, how to ask our questions while maintaining respect for the privacy of the student who has volunteered to be in the role of the research interviewee. I generally warn my students that the interview portion of data collection can be an emotional process, and meeting privately with the student "volunteers" ahead of time enables us to set up a "safety valve" in the form of a signal the student can give to the professor if they decide they do not want to proceed further.

"Do No Harm"

Some years ago, one of our outstanding psychology majors was running a support group for students who had been victims of sexual violence—in particular, date rape. She wanted to study the experience of date rape for her thesis, but we came to an agreement that it would be unethical to open up those experiences for the purposes of research, even if they had a support group to help them deal with the reawakening of trauma. The fact that the group was being facilitated by a fellow student who had been in the same kind of situation did not mitigate the fact that there was no professional there to turn to if someone were to become disturbed by their participation in the study. So, the focus of the study shifted to asking her participants to reflect on a recent dating experience, with an interest in understanding how their past might still be "present" in their social encounters. One set of data with three analyses by different researchers was eventually published as an exercise in both demonstrating the method of existential phenomenological research (EPR) and examining the reliability of the method (Churchill et al., 1998).

SELECTING PARTICIPANTS

Typically, it is important to select participants who are not only willing to prepare a written statement (wherever possible) but who will also be available for follow-up interviews for clarifications or elaborations of the data. Beyond the question of accessibility, we draw our participants from people who have clearly experienced the psychological phenomena under investigation and, most important, who can be articulate in describing their experience. In some cases (e.g., recent research we have conducted with immigrant informants), this may mean inviting participants to speak to us in their native tongue and then arranging for translation of their testimonies. The founders of our method always emphasized that we should draw our sample from "naive" participants, people who have not studied psychology or phenomenology; the idea was to ensure that their descriptions would be couched in descriptive language rather than concepts or jargon, to leave the analysis to the researcher.

It is not a question of convenience sampling, stratified sampling, or even random sampling (although we return to this issue in Chapter 7), but rather, we engage in a *purposive sampling* "for the identification and selection of information-rich cases related to the phenomenon of interest" (Palinkas et al., 2015, p. 533). Englander (2019) argued effectively that in phenomenological research, we are not so much looking at empirical "individuals" from within a finite "population" as we are sampling "meanings" from within an infinite "world" of possible experiences. In this sense, a qualitative study of "spinal cord–injured patients" becomes, essentially, an inquiry into "the world of spinal cord injury." Within the world of spinal cord injury, we have the world of the injured and the world of those related to the injured person, all of which gives us access to this particular "world of experience." This is why Giorgi's (2009) basic criterion for the selection of participants is simply that they have lived through the experience of the phenomenon being investigated (p. 122). That is because meanings are not like traits or variables that are shared by individuals who are a part of an empirical population; meanings are context dependent, and there is "no end" to the field of possibilities within which one might find examples of the meanings inherent in the human experiencing of a particular phenomenon.

As presented by Englander (2019), *population* is a technical term that has made its way into psychological research through the rise of statistics in psychology, and it has acted as a background for quantitative research methods (which are based on "probability sampling"). Hence, one could argue that it has no place within the "theory of science" of phenomenological methodology. In studying the experiences of a very limited number of individuals, we are not involved in a process of drawing a sample from an empirical population; nor are we interested in the individual's experiences as some kind of "empirical" evidence to be used in prediction. Rather, we regard the individual and their experience as exhibiting psychological "phenomena" that belong to "worlds of experience," and it is the latter that is our ultimate "object" of interest.

DEVELOPING AN EXPERIENTIAL "APPROACH" TO DATA COLLECTION

The process of doing EPR is by definition a process of allowing a psychological phenomenon to show itself to the researcher. Heidegger (1927/1962) observed, "The word [phenomenology] merely informs us of the '*how*' with which *what* is to be treated in this science gets exhibited and handled" (p. 59, italics in original). This "how"—for Heidegger, a "letting be" on the part of the researcher—is primarily an attitude, a posture, a pathway, a way of being in a situation, a way of encountering. Ultimately, it is a way of being present both to the informant and to the phenomenon revealed, which can be described as a mode of open-minded generosity and noninterference, where researchers have put aside any ideas they have about the phenomenon to allow the phenomenon to appear in its own way of manifesting itself. This "how" of phenomenology is indeed a research posture that depends by its nature on one's being able "to look-at" (*an-schauen*) a lived experience by means of what German philosophers have called "intuition" (*die Anschauung*) and its derivative "empathy" (for intuiting or "looking at" the experience of others, to be discussed later). This "letting be" and "allowing to show" (the very meaning of the Greek *logos*, as in "-ology") is an attitude that one assumes when collecting one's data by means of the EP researcher's chosen style of "facilitative presence," both to the participant and the phenomenon under investigation.

The role of the researcher is, in fact, an active one from the beginning. We begin with a methodological distinction using the Latin words *data* (given) and *capta* (taken). Laing (1967) noted that "the 'data' (given) of research are not so much given as *taken* out of a constantly elusive matrix of happenings. We should speak of *capta* rather than data" (p. 62). For centuries, philosophers and psychologists have used the term *data* because it corresponds to the "tabula rasa" (blank slate) theory of knowledge, which states that we passively "receive" information from the world without contributing anything in the process. For Laing, the use of the term reveals a blindness in researchers who use this term uncritically—they think that what they are calling their "data" are really simple "givens." However, Laing was saying that for psychologists studying persons, there are no "simple givens" or "bare facts." Technically speaking, we should (as phenomenologists) drop the term *data* from our vocabulary because what we are really doing is actively gathering meanings—"capturing" the data, if you will—and hence, Laing believed if we were going to call them anything, we should use the Latin term *capta* (that which has been selectively "captured" or "taken"). This "capturing of meaning" on the researcher's part would be true not only when reading verbal reports but also during the process of collecting them by means of the research interview.

Moreover, our acts of engaging ourselves with the "meanings" of others' experiences are not just something that we do in our heads. We bring our whole body with us to the encounter with our data. This pertains as much to our encounter with our research informants during research interviews as it does to our encounter with their words when reading written or transcribed data. EPR is, in its essence, a method of *participant observation* (see Englander, 2020, for discussion). We get a "feel" for what they are saying from their presence to us during the encounter. And we "feel our way in" to the stories they tell us through our resonating attunement with their words. This is, in fact, the meaning of the original German term for empathy (*die Einfühlung*), from the verb to "feel" one's way "in" (*ein-fühlen*). In some of his earliest phenomenological lectures, Husserl (1910–1911/2006) was developing his conception of an "empathizing perception" (p. 164) through elaborating empathy as a transcendental condition of our humanity as researchers that actually makes possible the appearing and "capturing" and eventually the "viewing" of psychological phenomena in our experience of others. We return to a discussion of the importance of this process for EPR in the next chapter.

DATA-GENERATING ACTIVITIES

The decision of whether to solicit written descriptions outright and then follow them with interviews for the purpose of clarification or whether to conduct the interview at the outset as the primary means of data collection depends on the nature of the project and how much time one has for transcribing recorded data. If the researcher only has "one shot" at collecting data, especially when one travels to connect with a participant or when access is limited by institutional review board (IRB) requirements or those of the facility where the participant might be staying, then conducting an interview might be the method of choice to be able to get everything at once. However, one would most likely need to be a seasoned researcher and already trained in nondirective interviewing techniques to pull this off without the need to go back a second time for follow-up.

Recommended Procedure for Data Collection

In my adaptation of the method that I learned from Colaizzi (1967, 1973, 1978), W. F. Fischer (1974, 1978), Giorgi (1970, 1985, 2009), and von Eckartsberg (1971, 1986), I find it better for first-time researchers to request a written description to be followed up with an interview rather than attempting to conduct a research interview from the outset to obtain data. One benefit is to allow participants time to focus themselves before starting to communicate their experience. By sending an email to the participant with a clear question, the participant can take time to "collect their thoughts" before responding to the challenge of describing their experience. They can think about what they want to say, instead of just starting to talk, as is likely to happen in an interview.

The most important benefit of beginning with a prompt for a written description is that it enables you, the researcher, to be able to spend time with the description, reading and rereading, familiarizing yourself with its contents, and beginning to jot down notes for questions to be asked later during a follow-up interview. This also gives you time to think about how to ask questions in such a way as to avoid influencing the participant or "leading them on" simply to give you what you are looking for. Nondirective questioning is often best. Exhibit 3.1 presents a summary of the process of facilitating the generation of data in EPR.

1. Formulating the Access Question

As stated in Chapter 2, the questions that we pose to our research participants are designed to evoke descriptions without telling the participant too much about what we are looking for to avoid a tautology where the researcher imposes a preliminary sense of what the findings will be before the data has even been collected. Our "access questions" are typically formulated as a way of inviting the participant to open up with regard to offering a description of a specified lived experience or situation that we believe will yield narratives that we can use to access our phenomena of interest. Indeed, to be sure that participants do not misinterpret our instructions

EXHIBIT 3.1. Flow Chart of Data-Generating Activities

- **Create an *access question* that serves as a prompt for participants to write a description of a lived experience.** Considerations here include focusing them on the situation they lived through and, when possible, pointing to the psychological phenomenon within that situation that serves as the research interest, if that has already been decided through review of the literature and/or piloting.

- **First impressions.** Before formal data analysis, the researcher reads the data carefully, looking for points of interest, identifying places along the way that need elaboration for the researcher to more fully place themself in the participant's shoes to better understand the experience and to ultimately perform an analysis of the experience through empathic identification with the participant, whereby their experience becomes a "vicarious experience" of the researcher (Spiegelberg, 1975).

- **Follow-up interview.** Conduct a face-to-face recorded interview where the participant reads their description aloud, offering spontaneous elaborations as well as responses to prompts from the researcher (based on first impressions). This interview is transcribed and then used as the principal data for the study.

by giving us, instead, their own "implicit theories" or "thoughts about" their experience, we ask them to describe their experience in the form of a story.

In some cases, the access questions sent to the various participants can be modified to determine which version of the question results in the best data. For example, in the study mentioned earlier (Rao & Churchill, 2004) that was inspired by Sartre's (1943/1956) theory of "the Other's regard" (pp. 340–400), the access question posed to the first participant was, "Describe in detail how you felt when an Other perceived you as being beautiful." By posing this type of question, we were calling on the woman to give an account of the types of feelings that were evoked by another person's perception of her beauty. However, it might also have limited the participant's description strictly to feelings. The modified protocol question posed to the second participant was, "Describe in detail an experience in which you were perceived as being beautiful by an Other." In contrast to the first question, this one used the more general term *experience* in hopes of eliciting a more encompassing response (one that might include perception, motivation, memories). In these first two questions, we chose to include reference to "an Other" (as the perceiver), thereby directing the participant to place herself on the receiving end of someone's gaze in an actual encounter. The third question, posed to the remaining participants, was, "Describe a situation in which you experienced yourself as being beautiful." We purposefully omitted reference to another person in this version of the access question because we did not want to influence the participant's description directly, although we anticipated that they would invariably draw on "the other" in reference to their apprehension of themselves as being beautiful. What we discovered was that we did not need to "suggest" the presence of another person (whether actual or imagined) in our access question for participants to make reference to others' perceptions of them in their experiences of being beautiful (Rao & Churchill, 2004, p. 5). Experimenting with different access questions in this way during piloting enabled us to learn that we could obtain the descriptions we needed with a minimum of "suggestion" in the access question. This then strengthens the perceived validity of the research findings (namely, that participants were not simply mirroring the question posed to them).

An important consideration is how to articulate these access questions for those participants who might be less educated, representing disadvantaged groups. In our recent investigations into immigrant experiences of acculturation, humiliation, microaggressions, and other topics, I suggested to our student researchers that they interview their participants in their native tongue to be sure each person understood what was being asked of them—but more important, so that the informants could express themselves more freely and faithfully. A preliminary meeting between researcher and participant would enable rapport to be established, and if the participants were able to write down their experience in Spanish, our Latinx researchers could then conduct the follow-up interviews in Spanish, translating into English for purposes of their report. (If reports were to be published, I would advise including the original language followed by translation for each unit of data.)

2. First Impressions

I suggest that researchers write down their "first impressions" while reading the written data for the first time. Here, you begin to pose your research interest to the data: You need to begin by first asking yourself what you hope to learn from your analysis of these data. What do you think is inherent in this description that you could successfully bring to light? These first impressions contain fresh insights, usually of value because they reflect the psychological themes inherent in the data that "jumped out" at the researcher on first encountering the data. It is the informality of these first impressions that makes them less intimidating to articulate in the first place. By writing down one's first impressions, these spontaneous (and potentially uncritical) thematizations can be "put aside" for later clarification and critical reflection.

3. Follow-Up Interview: Elaboration of Meaning Through Cooperative Dialogue

After reviewing the written description, the researcher then meets with the participant, preferably soon after receiving the description, so that the material is fresh in the informant's mind. It is best to be prepared with at least one, if not two, recording devices so that if one fails, you have the other as backup. Among the most common mishaps with the recording of interviews is the recorder not being turned on or turned on without the microphone picking up the voices or jamming in some way or running out of power. Having both a portable recorder and a smartphone recording the interview is advisable, given the risks involved in digital recording, where entire files can disappear or become corrupted.

One of the original and most incisive formulators of EPR, von Eckartsberg (1971), referred to this follow-up interview as a "cooperative dialogue" with our participant-informants. The researcher can never really assume that they understand what was said or written, so they have to obtain a clarification from the person studied. This is because "the protocol of experience as obtained in self-report" is never as rich and exhaustive as the original living flow of the experience (p. 77). "The method is hence dialogical and the researchers enter into a give and take with the [participant]" (p. 75). The researcher starts by asking the participant to elaborate on the meaning that the reported components of the self-report protocol have for the participant. This is important because it "allows clarification and specification of meaning—as the person studied himself experienced it—and it prevents importation of meaning from an 'alien frame of reference' on the part of the researchers" (p. 77). However, as von Eckartsberg astutely observed, "there is always a more personal and subjective meaning, constituted by the unique biographical experiential constellation and given to the awareness of the person, which remains largely unexpressed although it is [nonetheless] constitutive of the lived experience" (p. 77). For this reason, the researcher must pay close attention to the words, expressions, and meaning contexts of the informant during the interview.

Preparation for the Interview. You should develop your questions in advance of the interview by carefully reading and reflecting on both the written protocol and the notes taken down earlier as "first impressions." This enables you to try to find ways of eliciting elaboration without asking questions that are too leading (i.e., too specific). More often than not, just asking the participant to "say a little more" along the way can be enough to open up the data to elaboration.

Conducting the Interview. You begin by asking your participant to read aloud from their written description (also referred to as a *protocol*), inviting them to elaborate as they read. Any elaborations offered spontaneously during the interview are then considered part of the original data. This is particularly helpful in dealing with participants who write little in their first attempt. During the interview, you should ask the participant to pause at the end of each sentence (or elaboration) before moving on so that the researcher can interject questions prepared in advance, as well as those that occur spontaneously during the interview. Next, you make a transcript of the interview, which contains all the original written data, the spontaneous elaborations, the interviewer's comments or questions (necessary so that future readers can determine whether the researcher has induced the participant to say certain things), and the interviewee's responses to the researcher's questioning. The resulting transcript becomes the data for your subsequent analyses.

Researcher's Questions. Although some phenomenological researchers, such as Moustakas (1994), direct their trainees to prepare a list of questions as the main method of collecting data, the method prescribed here differs by leaning toward a more "minimalist" approach in the asking of questions. This is because our aim is less to collect information as our "findings" and more to provide a first-person narrative of meanings for the researcher to then reflect on to determine more precisely how those meanings arose in the experience of the participant.

Advantages of the Face-to-Face Follow-Up Interview. The interviewer should be sensitive to the interviewee while guiding them through the interview, be empathic where compassion is called for, and allow the time and space for interviewees to feel safe and comfortable to reveal themselves. The researcher who generates a warm, embracing quality within the encounter is sometimes rewarded with the most fascinating revelations. Although it is the "first-person" experience of the participant that is of interest to the researcher, the researcher's "second-person" perspective (insofar as they are addressed by the interviewee) provides a privileged position from which to observe the participant's self-presentation during the interview. (Elsewhere, I have developed this phenomenological notion of "second-person perspectivity" and its implications for both research and patient care. See Churchill, 2006, 2012, 2016, 2018a.) Clearly, the interviewer is a coparticipant in the interview. Some have developed this dialogal approach to data gathering into a variation in the method in which the data are generated by a team of coresearchers engaging in a group dialogue with each other about their phenomenon of interest (Halling et al., 1994, 2006). It is once more in this sense that the interview transcripts present not simple *data* but *capta* (in Laing's sense): The interview encounter becomes a place where understanding is engendered, and meaning is indeed captured (rather than simply "given").

One of our recent students (Ruiz de Somocurcio, 2016, p. 82) had this to say about the benefits of conducting an in-person interview with her participants:

> One advantage . . . is that their body language and facial expressions can be observed as they talk about the experience and this can be used as more evidence and be helpful during the analysis. Because an experience is lived with both mind and body, it is important to be able to look at these signs, and physiognomic expressions, that give a little bit more insight as to what the experience was like for that person (Giorgi, 2014, p. 246). But most importantly, conducting an interview about the data is the only way for the interviewee to "elaborate," and the interviewer to get more "clarification" and "specification" about the meaning (von Eckartsberg, 1971, p, 77). "Only in this fashion can [the researcher] safeguard against premature and falsifying interpretation" due to misunderstanding the data or having to assume things without enough information. (von Eckartsberg, 1971, p. 77)

Indeed, it is typically in the research interview that the researcher can begin to plumb the depths of a description, to move beyond what was said explicitly to what was at first only implied or revealed by the way that the body speaks through blushes, tears, grimaces, and smiles (see Churchill, 2010b, for further illustration).

The empathic grasping at meaning is already a part of the way phenomenological psychologists are present to the participant during the interview phase of data collection. And it is the essential component of the researcher's experience later during the data analysis phase, in which underlying meanings and significations are identified and elucidated. In both the interview and more solitary moments of data analysis, the phenomenologist is interested in not only what is obvious but also often, more essentially, what might otherwise go unnoticed.

An Example From a Classroom Follow-Up Interview. In a description written for a research class where the prompt was to "write a description of an emotional experience," a Latinx student we refer to as "Rosa" recalled a time when she was 14 and her junior high school teacher was mocking an African American classmate who was known to be clumsy and had fallen into the mud outside during recess. The teacher had a history of making fun of this particular student, and on this occasion, it became too much for Rosa to bear. She had characterized herself to the class as normally quiet and timid during her early teen years, and yet on this occasion, she found herself standing up, knocking her chair over in the process, and shouting at the teacher that she wished it was the teacher who had fallen in the mud and her that everyone was laughing about so that she would know how it felt. Part of what had made this an "emotional experience" for her was not only her feeling protective of her classmate but also her immediate awareness that she might be expelled from school for yelling at her teacher. All she could think about was how hard her parents had worked to bring them to America to have a good education, and now she was jeopardizing all of this in one outburst of emotion.

After sending Rosa out of the room so that the class could discuss what kinds of follow-up questions we might pose to her, we brought her back in and simply asked whether she had ever felt that way before. She nodded her head and replied that she had had some experiences when her family first immigrated to Texas. But then she went right back to the moment she had been describing and commented that none of her classmates at the time could believe that she, being so little, could make such a ruckus. There was some mild laughter in the room, and Rosa was smiling, almost proud of her story. There was a pause, our eyes locked for a moment, and I said to her, "You mentioned your family?" There was another pause. Her eyes began to well up with tears.

A classmate sitting next to her put her arm around Rosa, and through her tears, she related a story about how this moment of seeing her classmate ridiculed resonated with the way her family had been stared at and reviled by locals when they first moved from Mexico to their small Texas town and walked for the first time into a grocery store. As they walked into the small store, everybody in the store stopped what they were doing and just stared at them. Our class, with several Latinx students, sat in quiet solidarity with Rosa at this moment. Bringing her back to the emotional experience, I commented that it was like she was literally "taking a stand" in the moment when she knocked her chair over—standing up for her classmate and her family as well. Rosa replied, "I've never thought about that before. People always laugh when I tell them this story." There was some nervous laughter in the room. Still looking at Rosa, I asked, "We laugh in order to __?" Regaining her composure, Rosa replied, "I think we laugh in order not to feel the hurt of it all."

What beautifully came across to the entire class (and I was so appreciative of Rosa's generosity in sharing her story) was how the indignation described in her original description was just the surface of a more painful depth and that just below the anger and the indignation was the hurt that she carried with her, which the anger—and the laughter whenever she related the story—had succeeded in veiling. Rosa would tell me later that although this had happened 5 years ago, every time she told the story, she too had laughed about it. And it was not until this moment in class that she understood what her emotion was really about.

(Whenever these kinds of deeper feelings arise during workshop sessions, I spend time with the student immediately afterward to provide support or even a referral to our counseling center if warranted—though, to date, the latter has thankfully never been necessary.)

Further Reflection on the Researcher's Facilitative Presence

In terms of the tone of presence between the researcher and the interviewee, this attitude might best be characterized as one of *passive receptivity* and *empathic dwelling*—ways of being with the informant that invite them to further self-disclosure (Churchill, 1984, pp. 114–119; 1998, pp. 194–197). It is a way of listening that helps draw out the participant descriptions, observations, and reflections that might never have come forth on their own were it not for this inviting presence of the researcher. While being patient and empathic, the researcher can also actively engender a contemplative attitude on the part of the informant by simply slowing down and "dwelling" with their words. The researcher might take advantage of a pause on the part of the interviewee to smile supportively and say, "I wonder if there isn't more to it?"

I have come to realize that the gentle presence of the interviewer opens up a space of safety for the participants to reveal themselves, transforming the interview from an anonymous encounter to a more personal one for both parties. This facilitative posture of the researcher actually coconstitutes the generation of data. A participant would most likely not come forth with much in the way of deep reflections if simply asked to sit down and write a description of a moment of their experience. They will tend to give you a "matter of fact" account and be done with it. It is important that student researchers think of themselves as more than just passive recipients of information; rather, I encourage you to think of yourselves as engaged in a process of participant observation (Churchill, 1998; Englander, 2018, 2020; Sullivan, 1954; von Eckartsberg, 1971).

Whenever I teach the method, I try to teach students to look at both the surface and possible depths of the description. On the surface, we can often do no more than summarize or find more concise words for articulating our "findings." In getting at the deeper layers of an experience—"getting under the data," so to speak (A. Fisher-Smith, personal communication,

September 16, 2020)—we use a kind of listening to the words of our informants that is more contemplative—and hopefully more "receptive" than it is "imposing." Hearing deeper meanings, listening for significations—even what Heidegger called "hearkening"—might come into play here. One does not have to go far in attuning oneself to the data to connect with what Dilthey (1924/1977a) called the "secret" of the person.

SUMMARY

In this chapter we have introduced you to the process of collecting data phenomenologically, which includes conducting interviews to bring yourself closer to the experience of your participants. With a little bit of sympathy and imagination, we can go a long way toward bringing ourselves closer to the so-called inner life of the Other whom we are studying. To borrow a psychoanalytic expression, we have to learn to "listen with the third ear" (Reik, 1948). When listening in this way to the suffering of the Other, it is not that we are reminded of our own suffering; rather, we "suffer-with" as we bear witness to the Other. We might even become attuned to a suffering that lies just below the surface of the Other's expression, somewhere just out of their reach. But we feel it, we sense its presence, we know that it is there. To borrow Heidegger's phrasing, it is not revealed in "what is [actually] said in the talk" but rather in what we intuitively understand that the talk is "about" (Heidegger, 1927/1962, p. 205). Such understanding requires moments of "shared attunement" that occur quite spontaneously and which can be "cultivated"—but never "made to happen"—in the researcher's experience. (In this sense, empathy training can only go so far.) In this compassionate mode of understanding, we do not need to revert to our own inner world to understand the other; we remain curious and attentive to the others' "inner" world, which is now a "shared" world.

Once you have your transcribed interview prepared, you are ready to proceed to the next stage of EPR, which is data analysis. I present this process in the next two chapters as containing two phases, the first of which consists of focusing on moments within the whole experience, followed by the second phase of comprehensive synthesis, which amounts to a psychological retelling of the participant's story.

4 FIRST PHASE OF DATA ANALYSIS

Focusing on Moments Within the Whole

What are we actually "doing" when we read and reflect on qualitative data? What are the operative principles for our data handling and data analysis procedures? And, in what sense are we "involved" with the data—empathically, imaginatively, experientially—while engaged in our "method," which for the phenomenologist includes "intuition," "analysis," and "description" (Spiegelberg, 1982)? The emphasis in my presentation of method is on the experiential aspects of the reflective analysis performed by the researcher. In Chapter 2, I drew a distinction between the experience that is interrogated and the latent meanings that the investigation brings to light. The former was described as the "situation" to be explored via collected descriptions. The latter was described as the "phenomenon," as that which "appears" to the researcher through the words and self-presentation of the research participant. The data express the participant's experience as lived and reflected on by the participant: They compose the situation that is subjected to analysis. The findings express the participant's experience as understood through the researcher's analysis: The phenomenon emerges as the researcher's understanding of that experience. We must always bear in mind what the term *phenomenon* signifies both philosophically and

https://doi.org/10.1037/0000257-004
Essentials of Existential Phenomenological Research, by S. D. Churchill

scientifically: It means that something is being brought to the encounter with a consciousness in whose presence meaning becomes illuminated.

DOING PSYCHOLOGY PHENOMENOLOGICALLY

The researcher stands in an experiential relation to the "data" in this method of conducting research; the researcher can even be said to enter into an existential relationship with the experience under investigation (Colaizzi, 1978, 2001, 2002; Spiegelberg, 1975; von Eckartsberg, 1971). I emphasize the attitude within which we come to resonate with meaning discovered within the data. This attitude requires that we cultivate within ourselves a sensitivity to meaning, which comes from a culmination of one's lifetime of experiences, interacting with others, experiencing the arts, and reflecting on one's experiences and the contributions we make to those experiences. This means that there will be individual differences in the way data are analyzed, with different researchers often seeing different (though rarely contradicting) meanings. We have been able to demonstrate that there are plenty of convergences in the ways that individual researchers analyze the same data (Churchill et al., 1998). Phenomenologists resist the temptation to believe that the meanings they see are "actually" there as "simply given" in the data—such a belief is one more example of what Husserl (1913/1962) called "the natural attitude": the belief that the object of perception actually is the way it appears to me. We understand that in our research process, there is a coconstitution of meaning that takes place when a researcher reads data (written descriptions, interview transcripts) and then interprets ("grasps at the meaning of") what they are reading. Seeing, hearing, and grasping meaning require the researcher to be more than a "blank slate"— and more of a facilitative presence participating in the revelation of meaning. The researcher is engaged in a process of actively constituting a world of meaning.

Part of what is meant by "researcher reflexivity" (Finlay, 2003, 2017; C. T. Fischer, 1994; Salner, 1996) is that we try to be aware of the fact that we are always at some level coconstituting the meanings that we "find" in our data. This means that we are careful not to come to premature closure on the meaning of our data. We are always going back and reconsidering whether there might be a better way of capturing the sense of a particular passage of data. We bring the same critical perspective to bear in our reflection on our participants' ways of meaning making. The other's experience is "purified" of the self-deceptions that are often maintained in the descriptions provided,

EXHIBIT 4.1. Overview of the Process of Data Analysis

1. Preliminary familiarization with the participant and their data (Chapter 3)
   (a) Preinterview reflection on the original protocol
   (b) Conducting the interview
2. First phase of formal data analysis (Chapter 4)
   (a) Reading and reflecting for a sense of the whole
   (b) Division of the transcript into "meaning units"
   (c) Transformative reflections on psychological meaning
3. Second phase of data analysis: comprehensive synthesis (Chapter 5)
   (a) Individual structural description
   (b) General structural description

and in the ensuing analysis, the individual's participation in the generation of meaning is taken up and made explicit (Churchill, 2000).

Exhibit 4.1 presents each of the steps of analysis and synthesis presented in this book.

Preliminary Familiarization With the Data

The process of data analysis has already been set in motion when the researcher engages in their initial reading of the informant's written description of their experience, making note of first impressions, developing the follow-up questions, and conducting the follow-up interview (see Chapter 3).

First Phase of Data Analysis: Reflecting on Each Moment Within the Whole

This first phase of the data analysis consists of three discernable steps, each directed to distinguishable "moments" of experience revealed within the full transcript of data. An example immediately follows.

1. Reading and Reflecting for a Sense of the Whole

After the follow-up interview, when all the data have been transcribed, the researcher reads the entire protocol to get a sense of the whole. The addition of elaborations and clarifications during the interview process will have added various dimensions to the original written description, so the researcher needs to familiarize themself with this new form of the data, with an eye toward dividing the data into manageable pieces for subsequent analysis. Commenting on this process in her senior thesis, Watson (2016) reported,

> By spending time with the protocol as a whole before considering its constitutive pieces, I was better able to empathically connect with the participant's sense of the experience as a single unit. We do not experience life as an ordered progression of moments. Our experience is characterized by chunks of time that are connected by a single intentionality towards the [moment-by-moment] occurrences. To be true to the participant's own experience, I, as researcher, must begin my consideration of their protocol with the wholeness of their description firmly in mind. (pp. 33–34)

2. Division of the Transcript Into "Meaning Units"

To proceed with a rigorous and systematic approach to the data, there must be "no stone left unturned." To ensure this, Giorgi (1975, 1985) prescribed that every piece of the original data be carefully examined, one at a time: "Since one cannot analyze a whole text simultaneously, one has to break it down into manageable units" (Giorgi, 1985, p. 11). These components are identified by reading through the transcript more slowly, delineating each time that a transition in meaning is perceived with respect to the research interest of the researcher. That is, the discrimination into meaning units takes place "from within a psychological perspective and with a focus on the phenomenon being researched" (Giorgi, 1985, p. 10). These delineated meaning units exist in the eye of the beholder:

> It is important to note that we are not saying that the meaning units exist in the text *as such*. They exist only in relation to the attitude and set of the researcher. . . . What stands out depends very much upon the researcher's perspective. (Giorgi, 1985, p. 15)

Depending on the length of the transcript, discrete units of meaning are sometimes identified as phrases or sentences, or in the case of more voluminous transcripts pertaining to experiences that take place over a greater span of time, the handling of such data might require treating whole paragraphs as meaning units, each of which remains a component of the overall experience. Of course, there is no "actual" meaning unit apart from the researcher's "regard" that constitutes the phrase or sentence or group of sentences "as" a meaning unit. So, there is no "right" or "wrong" here, even if it turns out that there might be "better" ways of handling the data in this step. What matters is what helps to bring out the meaning inherent in the data. The meaning units are typically demarcated by using slashes (/) to indicate wherever a shift of meaning occurs, which then helps to shift the focus of the researcher's reflection during the next step.

3. Transformative Reflections on Psychological Meaning

In this next step immediately following the identification of meaning units, the researcher is posing some variation of this generic question: "What does this moment reveal about the participant's psychological interests (general orientation, intentionality) within the overall situation?" The ensuing explications of the data are written down informally as "researcher's notes" that articulate the participant's implicit contribution to how their experience unfolded. We call these reflections "transformative" because there is a shift from the participant's reporting the "facts" of the situation to the researcher's elucidating the meanings and intentions inherent in the situation.

It is important to note that our reference here to "steps" is best grasped as referring to shifting moments of reflection on the part of the researcher that sometimes can be happening simultaneously. Exhibit 4.2 is excerpted from a student thesis on immigrant humiliation to give the reader a sense of how these "transformative reflections" can be presented. For reasons of space, I only include two of the demarcated meaning units, each followed immediately by the researcher's transformative reflections regarding those units.

In the next section, I present in more depth the method for actually arriving at these transformations.

Grasping at Personal Meaning in the Data

In the meaning unit analysis, where individual moments of a person's experience are subjected to the researcher's reflection, I encourage informality when writing down one's psychological impressions of what is being revealed in the data. In my experience as a researcher, I have found that the notes I make to myself in writing down my "analyses" of the various moments of the participants' experiences are more like tracks left behind in the process of thematizing my results. They are not yet the final statements of one's analysis; rather, they represent approximations along the way.

However, there is value to the meaning unit analyses aside from their serving as researcher's "notes"; they are included in the report, wherever space allows, so that the reader can, as it were, look over the shoulder of the researcher, reading the data along with the researcher, and begin to "see" the process of elucidation unfolding in front of their eyes. The reader becomes aware of the researcher's "presence" to the data in the way the latter comments on the data, and in reading the results of a phenomenological investigation, the reader can begin to resonate not only with the participant's story but also with the hermeneutic relationship made manifest between the researcher and the words of the participant. The reader begins to see how elements of the researcher's "approach" to existential dimensions

EXHIBIT 4.2. "Spotlight on Transformative Reflections"

[MU 10: With time, I gained the courage to tell Alice that I wasn't going to keep cleaning the gallery for $100 and I commented to the receptionist that I was going to ask for a raise because I thought it was too much work . . . (R: "Before you went to ask for a raise, you mentioned it to the secretary?") Yes, we were talking beforehand and she knew how Alice treated me and so she asked me if I was happy with the job. And I told her that I really wasn't because it was a lot of work and that I was going to ask for a raise soon. And she told me 'Well let's see if she wants to give it to you.' I remember that when I hung up, I cried out of frustration and helplessness. I have lived here sixteen years and I had never felt so humiliated than I did with my experiences with that woman. I found myself frustrated, helpless and angry.]

Analysis 10: Blanca finally decided to take a stand against her oppressor, in a manner, by asking for a raise. In her own way, she was claiming that her work was worth more than she had been receiving and that it deserved its rightful merit. In a moment of trust, she confided in the receptionist about what she thought about doing, something that she had been afraid of the whole time before this point. In telling her, she reveals a need to feel encouraged and supported. But disillusion fell upon her when Alice called to fire her. The receptionist, who Blanca thought she could trust in, and who, she believed, understood and cared about her struggle ended up betraying her trust by telling Alice what was said. Feeling humiliated meant not only to be treated with less respect and dignity than she was worth, but also living the disillusion of others' lack of genuine interest in her pain and the inability to stand up for herself because of her migratory situation. Though she did not willingly remove herself from the situation Blanca recognizes that her situation was too painful to endure once more and instead of continuing the same pattern, she resolves to value her work for what it's worth despite the fact that she and her family might go through more financial struggles. The person that she wanted to be was someone whose work was valued for what it was truly worth and she could not be that person around oppressors like Alice, the receptionist, and Alice's parents.

[MU 14: I remember the last thing that my mom told me over the phone before she died. She said that she had already made her sacrifices for me (continues to cry). That it was my turn to suffer for my children. (R: "And those sacrifices that you've made . . . is it worth it?") Yes, it's worth suffering (stops crying). I see that my siblings have a career and their children too and they live in Mexico but they can't find jobs. Despite not being able to practice our career, our kids have a future. They can achieve their goals with their studies here, and it doesn't have to be a super high-paying job. If we give them support, they can improve their lives.]

Analysis 14: Having experienced those many moments of humiliation, Blanca finds meaning through her mother's words: that she too must suffer. She understands that as a mother she has had to and must continue to make sacrifices for her children. Because her future is no longer a future for herself, it is a future for her kids. Blanca's humiliation and suffering thus bear meaning not just in terms of experiencing her own humiliation and suffering through it, but also experiencing it for the sake of her children, just as her mother did for her and she honors that through her own sacrifices.

of lived experience (the researcher's "fore-having") comes to bear in the analysis of data. (See Exhibit 4.2.)

Characteristics of the Researcher's "Presence" Facilitative of the "Transformative Reflections"

I turn now to elaborate the reflective processes that make up the researcher's activity during this first phase of the research. We were already talking about the *doing* of existential phenomenological research (EPR) in Chapter 1, where I introduced Sartre's method of "purifying reflection" as a way of bracketing the cause-and-effect thinking of traditional psychological theorizing to allow a new view of human temporality to come into view. As we shall see in the following subsections, the "how" of EPR has much to do with our personal means of access: How do we make the experience "our own" so that we can then proceed to perform an intentional analysis on the other's experience that has now entered vicariously into my own? The question of access is there from the beginning, and it determines everything from the questions we ask to our mode of presence during an interview, as well as our way of engaging with the descriptions that we collect from our informants.

Empathic Dwelling

EPR requires that the researcher enters into direct, personal contact with the psychological event being studied. One brings oneself to the encounter with the research phenomenon by patiently "listening to" or "staying with" the participant's description. In doing so, one becomes ever more open to what is being communicated. Far from being some kind of intellectual attitude, this empathic listening is fully lived through the body. Husserl (1952/1989) observed, "In order to establish a mutual relationship between myself and an Other [*ein Anderer*], in order to communicate something to him, a Bodily relation . . . must be instituted" (p. 176). The ideal bodily relation here would be something like the face-to-face encounter, but in principle, one can institute a bodily relation to the other even if this relation remains one-sided, as in the case of reading self-report data or listening to a recorded interview. What is essential is that the researcher is capable of "coperforming" the other's intentional acts: "In empathy I participate in the others positing" (Husserl, 1952/1989, p. 177). To "posit" is to take a stand in relation to something, to "position" oneself in such a way as to illuminate certain meanings within one's situation. Thus, in empathy, I participate in the Other's positioning themself from a unique perspective within a situation. As noted in Chapter 1, Husserl described this transposition of oneself into the Other's situation as "trading places." In empathy [*Einfühlung*], while maintaining one's position as the researcher, one gradually allows oneself "to feel one's way into" the other's experience [*ein-fühlen*]. By means of this resonating attunement, one begins to understand the other's position within the situation described. This was beautifully illustrated in Exhibit 4.2, where the researcher wrote in her transformative reflection, "Blanca finally decided to take a stand against her oppressor, in a manner, by asking for a raise."

Concentrated Focusing and Disciplined Fascination

When one slows down and allows oneself to "dwell" with an entity or an experienced situation, details become magnified because there are fewer distractions on the periphery of one's consciousness. In this employment of intense interest, the researcher listens to every nuance of a participant's self-presentation with the aim of sensing possible significations. Single words or phrases open up constellations of meaning. As I become more and more absorbed in the world of the informant, there is an intended loosening of the hold I have on my own world. Through the discipline of concentrated focusing, I grow more toward resting in the "existential field" (von Eckartsberg, 1971) that lies between myself and the participant. I find myself wondering, "What does the participant mean here?" When I am fascinated existentially, it means that I am outwardly turned, or "standing-out" (*ek-stasis*), toward those aspects of my perceptual field that are most salient, which in the research situation, consists of the world of the informant. These imagined meanings erupt out of the "bodily felt sense" (Gendlin, 1978; Shapiro, 1985) that emerges when I am fascinated or simply moved by the participant's narrative. For example, in a fear protocol describing the experience of rappelling over a cliff, I found myself almost feeling a sense of vertigo while imagining what it might have been like to actually lean backward over a cliff with a 100-foot drop below me. The participant's experience became palpable to me in my "co-experiencing" [*Nach-erleben*] of the situation. This is what Dilthey (1927/1977b, pp. 128–135) referred to as one of the "higher forms of understanding" in the human sciences that enables us to grasp "experience-near" meanings. As a phenomenological researcher, I have learned to trust the spontaneous upsurge of understanding that occurs when I dwell meditatively within the field described or otherwise portrayed by the participant.

Every detail has potential meaning. On the surface, something may seem trivial, but this is simply what, to the researcher, does not at first make sense. It is trivial only if you make it trivial if you do not give yourself over to it. But it is precisely the hallmark of the phenomenological method that *everything* can be interesting in a psychological sense. Taking up the taken-for-granted and subjecting it to scrutiny results in the illumination of the meaningful within the mundane. For example, in a class research exercise where we read a protocol on test anxiety, the first sentence stated, "It was the first biology exam of the semester." When we divided the data into meaning units, nobody in the class initially put a slash after that first sentence, instead continuing to the second or third sentence before finding something "significant" or "meaningful." When I asked the class why no one had thought that the first sentence constituted a meaning unit, they were silent at first, until someone finally said, "Well, I thought you told us that sometimes the data are just giving simple facts that are not necessarily meaningful?" And at that point, another student, employing Husserl's (1925/1977, 1948/1973) method of "free variation in the imagination," pointed out that if he varied the statement to say it was the first history exam, theology exam, or philosophy exam, it really would not make any difference in the analysis of the informant's test anxiety. What was important was what came later in the data. I then asked the class whether it might matter if the student was pre-med. (This, in fact, turned out to be the case after the student who had collected the description went back to their informant and asked.)

At this moment in the seminar, I wondered aloud about the "self" that this informant wanted to be and the corresponding "world" that was to be realized. Here, I was using my imagination to open up the data. Perhaps this participant saw themselves as a future doctor who would care for their patients, who would realize themselves as a healer, who would inhabit the world of a successful doctor, living in a beautiful home, or perhaps choosing instead to work in the Peace Corps, helping humanity in other lands—either way, making their parents proud for all they would accomplish in life. All of this would be at stake if this person were to fail their biology exam; they might fail to realize themselves as the self that they wanted to be, and correlatively, they might fail to actualize the world of the doctor in their future life. The class began to see how the slightest of details in a protocol could be pregnant with potential meaning. "Disciplined fascination" thus means that the researcher must always "be on the scent" of meaning. In the elucidation of meaning that takes place under this attitude, the researcher is not limited to the participant's words but rather chooses those that best capture the participant's psychology. In the example in Exhibit 4.2, the participant simply stated, "I wasn't going to keep cleaning the gallery for $100," and the researcher's intuition filled in the rest: "Blanca finally decided to take a stand against her oppressor, in a manner, by asking for a raise. In her own way, she was claiming that her work was worth more than she had been receiving and that it deserved its rightful merit."

Deep Listening

Related to this concentrated focusing is something I call "deep listening" (Churchill, 2010a, 2018b)—a concept inspired by Heidegger's (1927/1962) notion of *hearkening* [*Horchen*], which for him is a deeper kind of listening, one in which we can even listen in silence (p. 207). Heidegger said that in the hearkening that comes from "dwelling" with the other, we are able to experience something of who the other person is through our deeply resonating mode of attunement to them. This hearkening requires sensitivity to one's attunement to the participant, as well as sensitivity to the participant's attunement to the situation in which they find themself. This sensitivity requires bracketing our "first-person" feelings in similar situations so that we can leave our capacity for "feeling" available to ourselves as our mode of resonating with the other's mode of being as revealed in the data. Our own subjective processes thus become "instruments" of our perception of others. Hence, we can only truly understand the other when we have been able to feel or suffer with the other (see Churchill, 2010b, 2016, 2018a, 2018b). A good example would be the one given at the end of Chapter 3, where the student told what was intended to be a funny story about herself during a research workshop, and our "hearkening" to her passing reference to her family provided her "emotional experience" of indignation with its existential depth. (Another example from a similar research class provides the central point of reference in Churchill, 2010b).

Intentional Analysis

To perform an "intentional analysis" requires that we focus on the "content" of a moment of experience as described to us, and then, having made this moment "our own" through empathy, we turn our attention from "what" is experienced to the "how" of our experiencing. By "how," I mean the manner in which we are directing ourselves toward the situation: What is at stake—how are we motivated—such that we experience "this" rather than "that"? In the jealous situation, how am I involved in the meaning making such that I experience jealousy rather than joy? A phenomenologist understands these meaning-making acts to be a function of the actor's "mode of presence" to the situation: the "how" that makes possible the experience as lived. The aim here is to thematize (in our imaginative uptake of the participant's experiential description) how we are standing vicariously in the situation such that we can imagine what our informant sees and experiences. Although it is certainly possible to see obvious meanings, phenomenological researchers are often searching for meaningful connections that are more "latent" within our experience. This idea of "leading ourselves back" from our starting point in the affairs of living to the deeper meanings inherent in those affairs is the meaning of what we have presented earlier as the phenomenological reduction. Phenomenological research is a matter of leading ourselves back (again, this is the meaning of "the reduction"— to "lead back," from the Latin *re-ducere*) from the experience as described to the intentional acts that enable the experience to be grasped as meaningful— that is, as signifying something "deeper" or "latent" or "implicit" within the flow of everyday experience. As I emphasized in Chapter 1, the adjective *intentional* does not mean "deliberate" but "implicitly purposeful"; it is a concept borrowed from philosophy that suggests that in our psychological life, we are always meaningfully oriented toward our world of experience, even if only implicitly.

This immanent teleological orientation, or "intentionality," is a way of acknowledging that even the simplest experiences always already bear the imprint of our meaning-attributing presence. The aim of phenomenology is to make this implicit activity explicit. Because we do not claim to be reading other people's minds, we try to check with our sources to make sure that the understandings we communicate about our participants' intentions resonate with their self-understanding. This does not mean that the participant is the final arbiter of the meanings described by the researcher, but it is generally the case that a good phenomenological characterization of the meaning of an experience is something to which people other than the researcher— including the participant—can attest.

This is one way phenomenologists regard latent meanings differently from psychoanalysts, insofar as the latter are not necessarily concerned with whether an analysand confirms the analyst's interpretation. Whereas, in the phenomenologist's grasping at meaning, fidelity to the phenomenon means starting with a fidelity to the experience as it was lived. "Latent" in-order-to motives, for example, when pointed out to the participant by the researcher, are typically confirmed by the participant in a kind of "a-ha experience," where the latent meaning rings true for the participant. (And if they do not, then the EP researcher should at least be willing to take a second look at their analyses.) At the end of our research, we generally share our findings with our participants for confirmation and further comment (see Chapter 7).

Illustration

Take the example of a jealous man. He observes his girlfriend across the room at a party, whispering to his roommate. He immediately becomes inflamed with jealousy; he "sees" that she is being unfaithful to him and, moreover, that his roommate is being disloyal. If we were to believe the jealous man's description of the situation, there would be nothing left to analyze; taken at face value, his description would reveal the "cause" of his jealousy: He was "made to be jealous" by the actions of his girlfriend and roommate. However, when we perform a "bracketing" of our belief in the actuality of what is taking place (Husserl's *epoché* of the natural attitude), then we are able for the first time to see the scene as a production of the jealous man's implicit beliefs rather than as a function of environmental variables. For all we know, his roommate and girlfriend could have been secretly planning a surprise birthday party for the jealous man. So, we bracket our belief in the factuality of what has been perceived and reported to us so that we might attend to something else—namely, how the jealously is constituted by the jealous man's desires, insecurities, and strategies for reducing anxiety.

The phenomenological psychologist thus aims to inquire into the "conditions of possibility" for the jealousy: On what basis, we ask, is the jealousy even possible in the first place? Is it on the basis of the fact that the roommate and girlfriend are whispering in the distance? Or does it perhaps have something to do with the jealous man's "project" to realize himself as the one who "possesses" his girlfriend or at least is assured of her affections? The psychological researcher's goal is to see our way back to those motivations, to those meanings or intentions that underlie our experience. We might wonder, for example, what would happen if the man in question were to experience relief rather than rage when he saw the two of them whispering. This imagined variation would reveal a change in the "structure" of the experience, one that would no longer be a viable condition for the possibility of jealousy because the experience of "relief" might suggest that his underlying (and perhaps unknown) intention was to free himself of this relationship. Hence, through this spontaneously produced variation in our imagination, we can get closer to the "meaning" of the jealous man's experience. If he is jealous, it is essentially because of his own motives in the situation—and not necessarily those of the others.

The phenomenological reduction brings us to reflect on how it is that the participant has construed things. It involves looking through the participant's eyes—not to affirm that everything is "in fact" the way it appeared to the participant but to be able to grasp through a resonating understanding how it came to be that this person experienced jealousy rather than something else. The suspension of belief in the "actuality" of the reported experience allows the psychological researcher to dwell in wonder with regard to the participant's psychological life, to what is "at stake" for the jealous man. It allows us to reflect on how our understanding of a person's "projects" in a given situation helps us to grasp the deeper meanings of their emotional life.

MENTORING EPR IN THE CLASSROOM: TRAINING THE RESEARCH TEAM

Spiegelberg (1975) wrote about taking a "workshop approach" in learning the phenomenological method. Although I treat this application in more detail elsewhere (Churchill, 1990, 2010b, 2018b), a few words here will help the reader to understand the value of being mentored into the practice of doing psychology phenomenologically. Researchers new to EPR tend to respond with eager fascination when being shown demonstrations of how a phenomenological reflection can penetrate from the surface of a description down to its deeper levels of significance to retrieve possibilities of meaning (Heidegger, 1927/1962, p. 437). We listen carefully to a fellow researcher's explication of meaning and ask ourselves whether we can see what *they* saw in the data. When we cannot agree, we raise an objection and then discuss the challenges involved in remaining faithful to the data.

Whether the aim is to train a group of researchers to work together as a team or simply to train individual researchers to engage in their own projects, this workshop approach can be effective in helping you as a researcher to identify your biases and habits of thinking that sometimes get in the way of a more productive and faithful analysis of data. When we talk about a phenomenological fidelity to experience (i.e., to our evidence), this means not going too far, but it also means that we must not simply reiterate the data. There must be some transformation, some way that your presence to the data has made a difference. One of the most illuminating discoveries during these workshops happens when we go around the room comparing the first impressions and meaning unit analyses produced by the various readings of the data. This is where the narrative aspect of EPR becomes apparent: Each student is essentially narrating the participant's experience in a way that differs slightly (but importantly) from the participant's narration. Some students do not go far enough and tend only to repeat or paraphrase the words of the participant; others go perhaps too far in overinterpreting the data. It is in the process of comparing the different researcher's retelling of the story, piece by piece, that you will learn from each other something about the range of possible "readings" of the data.

This workshop approach is something that researchers can employ on their own, even outside of a formal research class. Those of you who are not going far enough in culling meaning or significance from the words of the participant can see that there are other ways of rendering the data meaningful. Alternatively, those with a tendency to overinterpret learn from their peers that there are ways of saying insightful things about the data without going too far (where "too far" means saying things that other readers of the same data find questionable or simply ungrounded in the data). Going around the room and having each of you read aloud from your analysis enables everyone in the room to hear an almost "full range" of explications. Those who were initially shy might become bolder; those who were over-confident in what amounted to "interpretations" of the data learn to pull back a little. Hearing the sheer variety in the ways that even just a few of you can put into words your understanding of a common set of qualitative data opens up your imagination to more productive ways of approaching the research task. In doing so, you will be better prepared for your own "solo" projects.

SUMMARY

Phenomenological research is about "meaning making" on the part of both the participant and the researcher. The researcher's job is to improve on that meaning making by "seeing through" the surfaces of the description to what we referred to in the first chapter as "latent meanings." In this chapter, we have seen how the researcher acts as an active, facilitating presence to enter into dialogue with the data and begin to flesh out its meanings. To do so you must draw on all of your powers of understanding, tapping into the wisdom you have gained from your own experiences to shine a light on the experiences of others. Seeing meanings as they appear at the individual level is the first aim of phenomenological reflection. The next step is to achieve a synthesis of all these discovered meanings into a coherent whole.

5 SECOND PHASE OF DATA ANALYSIS

Comprehensive Synthesis

This phase of the research consists of formulating both individual and general "structural descriptions" that bring together all of the insights gathered along the way into a creative synthesis. (See Exhibit 4.1 for the overview of the process of data analysis.) At the simplest level, we can say that the individual structural description preserves those details of the original data that are considered "essential" to understanding the experience as it was lived. The researcher weaves together insights culled from the meaning unit analyses into complex sentences that express both the circumstances and the choices made. This would normally appear in the results section of the research; the meaning unit analyses are generally placed in an appendix as "researcher's notes." These structural descriptions are the most challenging aspects of existential phenomenological research (EPR) because it is here that all of the "point-by-point" reflections are integrated into a synthesis, first at the individual level for each participant and then at the most general level imaginable.

https://doi.org/10.1037/0000257-005
Essentials of Existential Phenomenological Research, by S. D. Churchill

INDIVIDUAL STRUCTURAL DESCRIPTION: A COMPREHENSIVE SYNTHESIS

Having intuited a sense of the research participant's lived experience and reflectively analyzed its meanings during the first phase of data analysis, the researcher next articulates the insights from their meaning unit analyses into an *individual structural description* (ISD) for each research participant. This ISD is essentially a final synthesis of the individual meaning unit analyses. This synthesis is an integrative statement that conveys the coherent structure of the psychological experience under consideration—its various constituents (e.g., temporal phases, existential characteristics) and their relations within the whole.

Seeing Interrelationships Among the Constituents

When phenomenological psychologists engage in presenting a synthesis of their findings, they are doing more than summarizing what is already in the data. (There are computer programs one can use if one merely wishes to summarize texts.) The synthesis of one's meaning unit analyses (discussed in Chapter 4) into structural descriptions requires that the researcher has, from the outset, an idea of what constitutes a "structure" or "synthesis" or "gestalt," and the best way for students to acquire a sense of this kind of writing is to steep themselves in the writings of existential phenomenologists such as Sartre, de Beauvoir, Merleau-Ponty, and Lingis.

Wertz (1985) had a helpful way of articulating what we are doing when preparing a structural description. In describing how the researcher sees the interrelationships of constituents within a whole, he wrote,

> The researcher addresses to each distinguished constituent, "What has this one to do with that other one, and that one, that one, and so on." Ideally each constituent is related to every other one. Another related question is "What has this to do with the whole; what place does it occupy and what contribution does it make?" Here, the researcher is attuned to coherence, the physiognomy of structure. In thinking through the togetherness and relations (for example, temporal, spatial, social) of constituents, the research[er] sees relative priorities, for instance that some aspects of the phenomenon depend upon or presuppose others in its overall structure. (p. 176)

Van den Berg (1972) observed that in structural description, "everything is mutually dependent and nothing comes first. No matter at what corner we start first . . . we always lift the whole carpet. Therefore, in principle, it is unimportant where we start with the description" (p. 109). Even if description might begin anywhere (in principle), it can make a difference whether one "frames" a discussion of the participant's relationship to their body (e.g., in an act of self-cutting) from the perspective of the patient's social relationships or whether we choose to reverse this "figure–ground" arrangement to reveal the patient's sociality as seen from the perspective of his or her self-cutting, which then presents a different "gestalt" to the reader. This is where the "relative priorities" referred to earlier by Wertz (1985) come to bear in the writing of a structural description; that is, although it may be arbitrary where one begins, one can also select the beginning point strategically—for example, to reveal the social meaningfulness of a bodily symptom (in the case of prostate or breast cancer) or the reverse, namely, the embodied expression of a dysfunctional social relationship (in some cases of bulimia). The beauty of van den Berg's impartiality with regard to the starting point is that it frees us to look in new and clever ways at the contingent and always interdependent relationships between self and world, body, others, and time (these four themes being general existential guideposts used in many phenomenological studies in psychology, pedagogy, and nursing science).

A Psychological Retelling of the Story

All of the relevant details of the original data should be preserved in what is essentially a psychological retelling of the participant's story. This new narrative is a retelling of the participant's story from your perspective as a researcher who has reflected on the deeper existential dimensions of the experience and woven those new insights into your structural description. In the ideal statement of results, the presence of the original data is so implicit that one should be able to read the results without having to read the data first. However, this can be quite a challenge, and in most cases, some kind of synopsis of the data should be presented in the research report before the statement of one's findings to ensure that the phenomenal nature of the data does not remain obscure to the reader.

Examples of structural descriptions can be found in some of the research studies listed in the references and appendix (in particular, Churchill, 1998, 2006; Churchill et al., 1998; Churchill & Wertz, 2015; W. F. Fischer, 1974, 1978, 1985; Rao & Churchill, 2004; Wertz, 1985; Wertz et al., 2011). Exhibit 5.1 is an excerpt from the same research I used to illustrate the meaning unit analysis in the previous chapter, this time presenting a synopsis and individual structural description drawn from all the data analyzed by this student for this participant.

EXHIBIT 5.1. Individual Structural Description

Refined Statement of Research Interest

I am interested in looking at the struggles of being an undocumented immigrant and coming to a better understanding of how immigrants cope with their circumstances.

Access Question Posed to the Participants

I am interested in the phenomenon of feeling humiliated, particularly that of undocumented immigrants. Can you tell me about one specific moment in which you felt humiliated? What was the situation? How did the situation or set of circumstances present itself, and how did you experience what was happening in that moment?

Idiographic Findings

The participant, Blanca Hernandez (pseudonym), shared several painful moments in which she felt humiliated. She revealed her interpretation of her humiliation and tried to make sense of her being in light of such experiences.

Data Synopsis: Blanca. Blanca describes how she felt underappreciated and belittled while working for a woman who exploited her because of her migratory status in the U.S. Blanca expressed how she felt taken advantage of and frustrated with her inability to stand up for herself. Blanca's encounter with humiliation was characterized by her boss's arrogant and condescending attitude towards her, which was especially emphasized in the presence of others. Her main focus, though, was having put up with such injustices out of economic necessity to support her family, her children being most important to her. Her description ends with the realization that the suffering and abuse she encountered is a sacrifice she made for the sake of her children and a hope for a better future.

Individual Structural Description: Blanca. Having believed that her life would be better upon immigrating to the United States, Blanca felt disillusioned when she found herself in economic need because the people she had begun to work for did not keep their word. When she started working for a woman who promised to find more work for her, she was again hopeful and believed that her situation was turning around for the better. However, she again felt disillusioned but also taken advantage of when she found herself trapped under the unfair and pretentious demands of this new boss who treated her with less respect than the rest of the employees, often demonstrating it in front of others. **To be humiliated for Blanca meant to be intentionally and publicly treated with less dignity and respect than others and to endure the abuse of people who believed themselves superior to her.** Finding herself stuck in this abusive situation became the backdrop for Blanca's humiliation.

Feeling humiliated meant that she was taken advantage of through her work. This experience is unexpected for her because she finds herself initially situated as someone who is deserving of respect and whose work is valuable and has in the past been recognized as such. She felt frustrated when she put her effort into being the best worker she could be and didn't receive acknowledgement for her work. On the contrary, she was faced with a condescending attitude from her employer who was unappreciative of Blanca's work and expressed her superiority over Blanca when she asked for her Green Card or Social Security number in front of others, promising to give her a raise as soon as she provided it. **Blanca's humiliation becomes heightened not only in the face of her boss's challenging and abusive attitude but also in the face of the receptionists' critical gazes and whispers, apparently knowing that she would not take a stand for herself against such injustice.**

However, she still lives with the pain of her humiliating experiences and in an attempt to alleviate the pain of her past, she does two things. **She transcends the humiliation by objectifying the receptionists as snakes.** In doing so it becomes easier to recognize

EXHIBIT 5.1. Individual Structural Description (*Continued*)

her unpleasant feelings towards them because it is more "acceptable" to admit to hating the actions of a dangerous animal. **She also desires that her main humiliator endure,** if not the same, then **a similar pain that she felt under her humiliation.** For Blanca, having knowledge that her employer had previously been fired from a job meant that she somehow had paid for the injustice done to Blanca. And while she doesn't explicitly articulate a desire to treat her humiliators as she had been treated, Blanca expresses satisfaction in knowing that her employer had been fired.

Despite knowing that her boss did not treat her fairly and was taking advantage of her work, she chose to continue working for this woman out of a necessity to alleviate her economic struggle. She was finding it difficult to make meaning out of her decision to come to the U.S. and even expresses a desire to leave in the face of her humiliation. It was hard for her to understand such encounters with her boss because **the person she understood herself to be prior to working for this employer was someone whose work was recognized as valued and appreciated.** She was also faced with a challenge to herself, a self that she understood as one who worked to contribute for her family; thus, she could not choose to escape her situation because doing so would mean that she was no longer the person she understood herself to be.

This experience became a turning point, fostering in her a sense of inferiority. She began to accept unfair treatment as normative as she faced others who degraded her work and took advantage of her. While she was able to question some of the demands from her other employers, she was unable to completely stand up for herself due to language barriers, shame, and fear. Her humiliation is deeply connected to the discrimination she faces. She comes to expect that all of her Caucasian employers will abuse their power *because* she is an immigrant. **She began to understand herself through the discriminatory lens of others, believing that being taken advantage of is something inevitable.** Like her humiliators, she justified their abusive attitude, attributing it to the fact that because they are citizens, they have more rights than she, or any undocumented immigrant does. Her "acceptance" of this was more a sense of resignation, which then cultivated her resentment against Americans. She finds herself in a tension of self-conflict as she continued to work for her employer. Despite her desire to be respected, she believed that it was not her place to demand respect if it was not given to her. As she recognizes that she *deserves* to be respected, she still seeks approval of others out of a desire to feel accepted. However, she is disillusioned when she realizes that their interest in her is not genuine. And even when she tried to stand up for herself, asking that her work be valued for what it is worth, she still finds herself unappreciated and helpless. **It is not until she reconstructs her understanding of herself as worthy of respect and fair treatment from others, despite her legal status, that she is able to move beyond her humiliation and take actions to protect herself from future humiliation.** Regardless of this, being an undocumented immigrant remains as a burden that she cannot overcome and that controls the way she comports herself with others. **She continues to be guided by the cultural, racial, and legal differences between herself and Americans even now, still expecting to be treated as an outcast.** Though being here for quite some time, she still does not feel completely welcome in her new home. She begins to come to terms with her humiliation and hardships as she comprehends them as sacrifices that she makes for her children. **Thus, living with the burden of being an immigrant becomes acceptable and thereby meaningful when she understands it as only a miniscule adversity to suffer in order to open up the possibilities for her children's future.**

Not all researchers will engage in EPR beyond the individual level. It is often the case that proceeding from the individual level of analysis to the general with the aim of making "knowledge claims" about the general level of analysis can add weeks and even months to a research project, especially at the dissertation level. The procedure of "free variation in the imagination" (discussed later), whereby every statement of findings at the individual level is subjected to reflective scrutiny—to check whether the findings still hold for "any or all" imagined variations of the experience investigated—takes a lot of experience and rigor to perform effectively. For this reason, I often recommend that first-time researchers (including my student whose findings were being used as illustrations here) set their sights on presenting knowledge claims ("findings") only at the idiographic level—and reserve their considerations "toward a more general understanding" for the discussion section of their reports to be presented as "implications" of the idiographic findings. (It is certainly good to "aspire to" external validity, even if researchers are unable to claim that they have actually achieved it.) That is, EPR can be effectively used as a kind of "case study" method to open up meaning at the individual level while awaiting exposure to more data to enable a better starting point for making more generalized knowledge claims (Churchill, 1990, 2013, 2018b; Wertz et al., 2011).

The move to a more general level of analysis requires both experience and deep insight into how unique experiences can nonetheless be understood as "variations on a theme." Ultimately, this "understanding rests on a special personal giftedness" (Dilthey, 1927/1977b, p. 135), one that we can certainly learn to cultivate. This aptitude for seeing "forms" of experience manifested in particular circumstances begins with learning to recognize themes that are common among several examples (see Garza, 2004) and eventually enables us to "lift off" imaginatively into the realm of the infinite (Natanson, 1973).

GENERAL STRUCTURAL DESCRIPTION: THE INTUITION OF ESSENTIAL MEANING

Researchers now face the task of bringing all the results together into a statement that articulates those characteristics revealed at the individual level that would hold true for any or all variations that one could, in principle, obtain empirically or produce via fantasy. This movement from individual to general levels of analysis is carried out by means of two essential steps as defined by Husserl throughout many of his writings from 1913 through 1938: *eidetic reduction* and *free variation in the imagination*.

As stated earlier, this reference to "steps" should not be taken too literally (that is, in a chronological sense). By this, I mean that one does not "first" bracket preconceptions and "then" try to see essential characteristics at the individual level, "followed by" performing free variation to arrive "finally" at general or even universal findings. Rather, one finds oneself inadvertently shifting between idiographic and nomothetic "levels" of analysis, as well as between efforts to see the phenomenon directly and efforts to "hold back" when ideas from elsewhere begin to spontaneously intrude. All of this takes place within the spontaneous flow of reading and reflecting on the data. Likewise, "empathic dwelling" with the data, "amplification" of meanings, "hermeneutic" reflection, and researcher "reflexivity" do not constitute a series of steps within a process but, rather, represent shifting moments in the researcher's experience; and, hence, they are better thought of as intermingling possibilities of reflective experience that can even occur simultaneously rather than as steps, stages, or levels of analysis.

1. Engaging in Free Variation in the Imagination

Here, one alters one's attitude toward the empirical data in such a way that the data are no longer of interest for their own sake, insofar as they reveal peculiarities at the idiographic level, but rather, they become of interest as a starting point for an (in principle) infinite series of variations by means of which the researcher tries to "see" a unity of sense, or *eidos*. Husserl (1948/1973) likened this "seeing of essences" (*Wesensschau*) to grasping a Platonic *idea* (p. 341). That is, in reflecting on all the data, we ask ourselves, "What is the 'idea' or 'form' that defines and unifies the varying 'content' found among the different descriptions situated in individual life experiences?" As Husserl (1948/1973, pp. 340–344) put it, when we "run through" a plurality of instances in our consciousness, a "unity of sense" becomes apparent. This unity of sense is the *eidos*—the "idea" or "essence" for which we are striving in our move from individual to general levels of structural understanding.

Concretely, we take the ISD produced earlier in this second phase of data analysis, and we read through it again, posing this question to ourselves: "What *kinds* of experiential phenomena have been represented in each of the moments depicted in the individual structural description?" We vary the phenomenon in our imagination, asking ourselves whether certain features of the experience presented in the ISDs could be eliminated without changing the essential nature of the phenomenon. Those features that appear to the researcher as the invariant or "essential" characteristics become the focus under this "eidetic reduction" (see Churchill, 1998, pp. 189–190). Here, it is a matter of sifting through the ISDs, eliminating the details of the experience so that only its most general schema remains. If the first "phenomenological" reduction "reduces" our attention (or "leads us back") to focusing on just the phenomenon as it appears (by bracketing preconceptions), this second "eidetic" reduction leads us back even further to what is essential to the phenomenon by bracketing what is inessential. You can see here how the *epoché* and reduction are interrelated while representing distinguishable moves within the researcher's consciousness: the one clears the way for the other. Bracketing, here, takes the inessential (accidental details) out of play; the reduction, in turn, focuses our attention on the essential (the invariant meanings that appear across all situations, real or imagined).

Among the best examples for readers new to this method is W. F. Fischer's (1974, 1978) studies of being anxious and Wertz's (1985) study of being criminally victimized. For our purposes here, I draw from W. F. Fischer's (1974) first effort to articulate an essential structure, using just one of his four paragraphs. What is nice about this early study for the researcher who is new to the phenomenological method is that the author takes the reader by the hand through both individual and general structural analyses, presenting his analysis step by step as "a" way of doing a phenomenological analysis. Unlike his subsequent analysis (W. F. Fischer, 1978) or the ones performed by most other researchers (e.g., Wertz et al., 2011), W. F. Fischer here articulates the structure in the "first person," using "I" instead of a third-person pronoun, thereby rendering the eidetic structure less "abstract" and more personal (and palpable) to the reader. W. F. Fischer (1974) wrote,

> Initially, becoming and being anxious in the above-described situations means being suddenly distracted, even torn away from my everyday, unreflective orientation towards and involvement with the people, things and possibilities of my world. No longer able to attend undividedly to whatever I was doing, I am momentarily suspended in my living; there is a kind of inarticulate confusion. Breaking through this, my body or parts thereof, intrude themselves and call me to discover and immediately understand their affected, alien suchness. I find myself moved to "see" myself, to bear a critical, evaluative witness to the me that is now congealed and totalized in the threatening meanings of a particular emergent possibility. In being anxious, I am unreflectively impelled to do something, to perform some self-saving act that would cut through the encroaching oppressiveness and would enable me to regain my world. (pp. 418–419)

In his later rendering of this "general structure," W. F. Fischer (1978) reverted to the more common third-person style of presentation. However, this use of the first person in the version quoted here helps the reader to see that in engaging in the "seeing" of essences, we can be so personally involved in our acts of reflection that it feels almost natural for us to lapse into the first person while articulating a structure that has begun to exist for us in our own experience as researchers.

2. Preparing Condensed and Illustrated General Structural Descriptions

After reflecting on all the statements in the ISDs in this manner of "free variation in the imagination" (just illustrated), the researcher prepares a general statement articulating the phenomenon at its most general level. They can prepare two different kinds of *general structural description* (GSD): (a) a condensed GSD (like the one presented earlier by W. F. Fischer, 1974) or (b) an illustrated GSD, in which the general findings are formulated in such a way that the illustrations are selections from the data that served as the basis for the eidetic reduction and free variation (for illustration, see Churchill, 1998, 2006). In this latter case, the presentation of results follows a hermeneutic approach "in which a structure, a system of order, is derived from the instances, and which serves to unify them as parts of the whole" (Dilthey, 1927/1977b, p. 138).

In this final step of EPR, the researcher produces a more generic statement of findings that is similar to the "themes" presented in other varieties of qualitative research—except that, if produced properly, these "kinds" of characteristics are so purely seen that they can fit virtually any variation that the researcher (or reader of the study) can conjure, either from memory or imagination. Similarly, Colaizzi (1973, 1978), W. F. Fischer (1974, 1978), and Giorgi (1975, 1985) have described a phenomenological "structure" as a description that transcends the details of the particular situation while at the same time articulating characteristics that would be necessary in every case encountered. Importantly, the term *structure* (when used as shorthand to refer to the findings in EPR) does not simply mean "description" but rather a "structural description" in which each component is mutually implicated with the other components within the description. Giorgi (1970) put it even more forcefully: In a structural description, the term *structural* means that each of the thematic findings is shown to be related essentially to the rest of the themes or dimensions of the experience uncovered in the research (pp. 178–184).

To bring this to light, I share in Exhibit 5.2 the tentative "general findings" of the study of immigrant humiliation prepared by our student whose ISD was presented earlier.

EXHIBIT 5.2. General Structural Description

Illustration of GSD

Toward a General Structural Description of Immigrant Humiliation

A situation of humiliation for an undocumented immigrant is one where an individual faces an intentional threat to his or her own sense of respect and dignity. This situation can present itself in many different forms because humiliation can be felt from individual to individual, from individual to group, or from group to individual. An experience of humiliation begins with the understanding of the self as worthy of respect followed by a recognition that such is not the way others will comport themselves toward them. Humiliation for an undocumented immigrant is contingent on their perception of the other's **purposeful intention to establish superiority while taking discriminatory actions against the individual.** Thus, the individual feels a threat to his or her safety and often falls into desperation because of a lack of courage to stand up for themselves. However, I can imagine a situation in which an individual feels indignation in the face of his humiliation and stands up for themselves, whether physically, verbally, legally, or any combination of the three.

The situation itself is significant because the individual already feels like an outsider and set apart from others, being an undocumented immigrant. This reinforces their feelings of a lack of acceptance. But it is also imperative to note what the individual understands the situation to mean. For humiliated undocumented immigrants, this **means facing a world that overlooks their needs to be recognized and treated with respect.** The humiliated individuals gradually come to expect that the treatment they receive will be different to others, particularly those who are not undocumented immigrants.

This humiliation involves a shift in a perception of the self, as individuals who are deserving of respect and appreciation, to individuals who only deserve respect from certain people. Individuals then come to expect unfair and discriminatory treatment from their oppressors and those like them. This can be accompanied by an uneasy feeling of regret. While some are able to take a stand against their oppression, others understand themselves as having no choice but to endure their humiliation, despite believing that they do, indeed, deserve to be treated with respect. Their possibilities for a better future are thus compromised, and humiliated individuals come to question their choice for leaving their home country and often desire a return. The discriminatory actions taken against the individuals engender resentment and hate toward their oppressors. **Often, whether implicit or explicit, the humiliated person expresses a desire for justice; this can either be an action for which the individual takes the initiative or can be something that happens along the way that the individual attributes as justice being served for the oppressor's condescending attitude.**

Note. From *Understanding One's Adversities as Meaningful Sacrifices: A Phenomenological Inquiry Into the Humiliation of Undocumented Immigrants* (pp. 30–31), by G. J. Mena Ibarra, 2016, unpublished senior thesis, University of Dallas. Copyright 2016 by G. J. Mena Ibarra. Reprinted with permission.

A genuinely phenomenological "general structural description" would be distilled down to only what is essential—that is, to those characteristics that have to exist in every imaginable case. Therefore, any characteristics that are there in some cases—even if representing all of the sample— but not there in every imaginable case would not then qualify as general phenomenological findings. Identifying empirical commonality is not the same thing as engaging in the "seeing of essences," insofar as the latter would, in principle, transcend any empirical limits. Each sentence of a phenomenological structure needs to characterize every empirical or imagined instance where the phenomenon does or might occur. It is the most difficult thing to prepare because it requires, to paraphrase Husserl (1913/1962, 1948/1973), a reflection that reaches toward the infinite.

Nonetheless, engaging in "the intuition of essences" by means of "free variation in the imagination" is one of the most interesting and enjoyable aspects of this method. If the reflection on individual experiences and meaning making on the part of our participants provides us with a vicarious glimpse into the lifeworlds of others (as seen in Chapter 4), the move to general insight provides us with a challenge that is hard to resist. What insights from the individual analysis can be carried over into our "grasping at meaning" at the most general level? And given the richly nuanced meanings revealed at the individual level of analysis, how much of this richness can we preserve in our formulations of what we believe remains true across all possible manifestations of the psychological phenomenon being researched?

This remains the final challenge for the existential phenomenological researcher—namely, to engage with the task of writing up one's findings in a way that will be coherent and compelling to the reader.

SUMMARY

We have seen through our illustrations how the intuition of essences and the formulation of general findings are based in part on the personal giftedness of the individual researcher. W. F. Fischer's (1974) GSD, though written in the first person, was able to achieve an impressive degree of generality in light of the years he had spent already reflecting on the phenomenon of being-anxious as a professor. Mena Ibarra's GSD represented her first solo foray into phenomenology, having been previously mentored in a classroom workshop experience (like the one described at the end of Chapter 4). Insofar as she knew the experience of humiliation firsthand from her own family's immigration experiences, there was a little bit of autoethnography going on here, as part of her "having been there before" in her own life experience. In addition, she benefited from being in a cohort of Latinx students who opened up to each other outside of class, where there was a good deal of solidarity and mutual support. Mena Ibarra's reading of her data became a way for her to crystallize a collectively emerging self-understanding among students from immigrant families in her class.

There was something of Halling et al.'s (1994, 2006) "dialogal phenomenology" and Spiegelberg's (1975) "cooperative research" at work here, even if only in the background, providing a deeper fore-having from which Mena Ibarra was able to see more clearly the themes emerging from the data. As Spiegelberg observed, "by entering sympathetically and empathically into one another's perspectives and by pointing out overlooked aspects of the phenomena" (p. 25), researchers engaged in collaborative workshop experiences are able to transcend their limitations in coming to ever richer understandings of their phenomena of interest. The move toward a general structural understanding of humiliation was a challenging one, given all the cultural contexts throughout the world within which humiliation bears its mark, its own brand of suffering. To acknowledge the limitations of her GSD, Mena Ibarra (2016) placed it in the Discussion section (rather than Results) in a subsection titled "Towards a General Structural Description" (p. 30).

The findings of your research investigations will need to be situated within the context of your literature review, method, and discussion. Methodological integrity requires you to make sure that each component of your research report aligns with all the others. We turn to this in our next chapter.

6 WRITING THE RESEARCH REPORT

The previous chapters bring us to a final consideration with regard to the research process, which is the task of communicating one's research journey and one's research findings to an audience. As qualitative researchers, we are narrators and meaning makers, and thus, in formulating our literature reviews, philosophical approaches, data analyses, and findings, we are truly engaged in a task of storying, of weaving a narrative of the series of events that have preceded us, inspired us, and grounded our work.

Given the nature of the process of conducting existential phenomenological research (EPR), where our data analysis is informed by our literature review, as well as by our "approach" to the psychological, there is the possibility that we shall understand our research interest, as well as our approach to the subject matter, better at the end of a study than at its inception. Especially for first-time researchers, the whole procedure might begin as a hypothetical endeavor ("What if I were to try to use this method to study something like this?"); but, by the end of the research, the student will have gained their own "lived" understanding of the process. Thus, the literature review and method sections as they appeared in earlier drafts might need to be reformulated at

https://doi.org/10.1037/0000257-006
Essentials of Existential Phenomenological Research, by S. D. Churchill

the end of the investigation. It is almost always the case that the procedure has been modified—that is, adapted to contingencies discovered within the data—and the researcher should now have an improved understanding of the procedure employed.

INTRODUCTION SECTION

In the Introduction, reformulate your research interest in a way that takes advantage of what you have learned in doing the research. In the first paragraph of your research report, get right to the issue being explored as you now understand it. Thus, the way you refer to your research interest (or research question) in the final report may change from how you initially conceived it. Methodological fidelity within EPR includes this honesty in letting readers see how, for example, the process of interviewing one's informants might result in alterations of the research aims.

In the Introduction section, the literature review should include only material pertinent to developing your research question. It should be organized hierarchically (following the American Psychological Association [APA] *Publication Manual* edition that is current at the time of writing, now the seventh edition, 2020), with clearly defined headings and subheadings. It should begin with an overview of what areas of literature are to be presented, their order of presentation, and the rationale for their inclusion in the literature review. Following the formal review of the literature, there should be a culminating statement of your refined research question in light of insights gained from your review of the literature. Think of this "refined statement of research interest" as a place where you offer the equivalent of an "operational definition" of your research interest by stating the "take-homes" from each area of the review, in terms of how that literature is now a part of your "fore-having" (Heidegger, 1923/1999, pp. 65–70; 1927/1962, p. 191) as you move into the process of data analysis.

METHOD SECTION

In the Method section, state clearly how you carried out a phenomenological investigation of your proposed topic. Method sections are critical in any research report and should be fully developed in a sophisticated manner, with subsections on the method of involvement of researchers in data collection, interviewing, reflexivity, and most importantly, presenting the definitive aspects of the method of reflection on the data that makes the work truly phenomenological (rather than some more general mode of qualitative research).

In claiming that your research is "phenomenological," you need to be able to say, first of all, how you were able to make the research phenomenon accessible to your direct intuition: How did you find a way of bringing yourself to the encounter with the phenomenon? Here you should draw on the vast foundational and methodological literature of phenomenology— both primary and secondary sources—to give your research its distinctive character as a work in phenomenological psychology. The mere fact of collecting self-report data does not define one's work as phenomenological; this merely qualifies it as qualitative research. It is in your method of interviewing and your method of analysis that your work can be truly recognized as phenomenological. For the sake of methodological integrity, you will want to identify the extent to which you used empathy, intuition, bracketing, phenomenological reduction, and imaginative variation while reading and analyzing the data. I encourage you to put as much as you can into your own words.

The Method section ideally would include two main subsections: "Approach" and "Procedure." The Approach is like a second literature review, except this time presenting the literature of existential phenomenology as the philosophical underpinnings of the method before presenting the qualitative procedure itself. In a similar way, the first chapter of this book presents what the reader needs to know in terms of our approach (or "theory of science"), before going on to the more procedural aspects of the method in the next several chapters. And like the first chapter, your Approach section would be divided into subsections covering what you consider to be the important conceptual foundations of EPR. It is best when your approach also addresses how each theme has implications for your specific topic. Here, you would articulate how you faithfully took up a "phenomenological attitude" in encountering the phenomenon: in your conceptualization of the questions to be asked, interviews with your participants, and reflections on their data.

The Procedure should be broken down into at least two subsections: (a) "Data Collection" and (b) "Data Analysis," with the latter broken down further into sections with paragraph headings indicating the steps you followed in performing the analysis. Again, you should be sure to present the reader with your own formulations of the reflective steps and not simply quote from sources. I encourage you to speak in your own voice when presenting your understanding of what you did to engage with the data. The Procedure section should be written in the past tense and read like a recipe for how someone else could engage in specifically "phenomenological" research.

RESULTS SECTION

The most important aspect of the research report is the presentation of results. The phenomenological principle of description (vs. explanation) points the researcher in the direction of attempting to create a richly nuanced, idiographic "thick" description of the event as it was lived. Original protocol data are sometimes not long, in which case they can be presented in the Results section and set off from the rest of the text by using italics and/or single spacing or some other convention of your choosing. If your data are too long to be conveniently included in the Results section, you might prepare summaries of the data so that the reader has a clear sense of your empirical foundation. These "synopses" can be presented just before the individual and general structural descriptions (see Exhibit 5.1). The actual meaning unit analyses can be placed in an appendix as "researcher's notes" so that readers can trace the analysis presented in the results section to the portions of data from which they were derived. The results should only present what the researcher is willing to stand behind as "knowledge claims."

Indeed, one of the decisions that researchers must make is how much of one's analysis can be considered genuine knowledge claims. Certainly, the idiographic findings from the meaning unit analyses used to formulate individual structural descriptions are presented as a part of one's formal "results." The question with regard to one's general findings is whether one has really performed free variation in the imagination in the production of a general structural description. Without being mentored by someone already trained in the phenomenological method, one generally cannot be sure that one's "general" formulations are to be included as knowledge claims. For this reason, I suggest to first-time researchers that you might concentrate your knowledge claims on the idiographic aspects of your research and discuss the general findings as "tentative implications" of the idiographic findings. By making the general findings a part of the Discussion section, it frees the researcher from overstating the reach of their findings (and possibly putting their credibility on the line). Sometimes less is more with regard to knowledge claims. That said, the ideal of EPR would be for general findings to be more precisely formulated—that is, based on a more rigorous (and mature) reflection so that the move from the individual to the general levels of validity can be confidently presented within the Results section.

DISCUSSION SECTION

In the Discussion section, address issues raised in the Introduction in light of your findings. According to APA Style, the first paragraph of the Discussion section should be a summary of the research project, almost like an abstract, including a brief characterization of the procedure and general findings, which then leads into a more detailed discussion of the study's relevance. In the Discussion section, you present the final and best state of your thinking on your topic—what you understand after you have worked long and hard to put this effort together. Here, it is important that you do not substitute a summary for a discussion. Certainly, there can and should be a "return to the literature" where you enter into an informed dialogue with some of the authors whose ideas helped shape your project. Referring back to the gaps found in the literature, areas of ambiguity, as well as ideas that you wish to contest now, in light of your findings, enables you to take your place at the table, so to speak, on the basis of your research and "speak back" to those who informed your study. Finally, limitations of the method are important, after which the implications of one's findings for theory or practice can be presented.

SUMMARY

In presenting the four components of a research report, I necessarily discussed them one at a time. However, it is important for the entire report to cohere in a way that is not simply a function of each section being written sequentially as the project proceeds from its inception as a research proposal to its completion in a written report. The whole should be more than the sum of its parts. To this end, you should try to go through and revise each of the components of your final report in light of the insights you have gained along the way. The findings of the study can help you to make more precise the review of the pertinent literature; they can also be used to sharpen the refined statement of research interest presented at the end of your introduction section. The final report should, therefore, not read as a slightly modified research proposal with the simple addition of results and discussion but rather as a statement written entirely from the point of view of the final result. It may even be the case that arriving at the end of your study might inspire you to completely recast some of your earlier draft material.

7

CONCLUSIONS

As in the case of all research investigations, researchers who use existential phenomenological research (EPR) begin with the judgment that our state of knowledge is in some way inadequate or limited. For example, fragmentary or contradictory theories, inconsistent findings, problematic methods, or scarcity of research about a particular subject matter motivates researchers to investigate certain topics. Phenomenological research is appropriate when an assessment of the literature leads to the conclusion that our existing knowledge is not sufficiently grounded in description that is faithful to some area of human experiencing, along with the belief that such a description will better our understanding.

Phenomenological questions are those that ask about the meaning or essence of what people live through—that is, about its basic constituents and types, how it unfolds over time, and so on. Once these research questions have been adapted and reformulated to the kinds of "access questions" that can be posed directly to naive participants, self-report data are collected and then analyzed according to reflective principles and procedures (see Chapters 2–5).

By taking notes as the analysis proceeds, the researcher begins to express their ongoing insights regarding the research question(s), and these meanings

https://doi.org/10.1037/0000257-007
Essentials of Existential Phenomenological Research, by S. D. Churchill

may be incorporated into the final synthetic understanding expressed in the research report. Ideally, all the participants' statements in the ordinary-language descriptions relevant to the research problem are addressed in the researcher's psychological descriptions, and all of the researcher's knowledge claims refer to evidence intuitively given in the data. The implications of the new knowledge may then be drawn out, including how it helps resolve theoretical controversies, new questions, and/or practical problems.

THE PLACE OF PHENOMENOLOGY WITHIN THE QUALITATIVE TRADITION

Perhaps because qualitative analysis of self-report data first emerged in the 1960s to 1970s within the field of American phenomenological psychology, various useful aspects of phenomenology found their way into other qualitative methods by a process of *sedimentation* (Schütz, 1970, p. 322), which occurs when formal ideas have sifted down (or "sedimented" themselves) into everyday (and even scientific) discourses. This process of sedimentation obscures the origins of these ideas and makes them seem natural and even obvious (Berger & Luckmann, 1966, pp. 104, 138, 163; Nichols, 1981, pp. 1–2). For example, the term *bracketing* (namely, holding back assumptions and biases during the analysis of data), which appears in many qualitative methods, was introduced by Husserl (1913/1962) with his concept of *epoché*. And yet, one is hard-pressed to find a citation of Husserl when qualitative researchers from outside of the existential phenomenological (EP) tradition talk casually about their "bracketing" of biases and preconceptions. Another term that comes directly out of phenomenology is *empathy*, used quite innocently by qualitative researchers to describe their facilitative approach to the participant during the interview. However, the term *empathy* (*Einfühlung*) actually came out of the German philosophical tradition (Lipps, 1903; Stein, 1917/1989) and was incorporated into Husserl's phenomenology as a "bridge" between self and other, one that enables us to have access to other "I's" and to the intentions emanating from those I's by (quite literally) *feeling* our way *in* [*ein-fühlen*] to the embodied life of the other. For Husserl, empathy does more than just establish rapport; it provides us with a form of "evidence-giving" that is on the same order of validity as our "sense perceptions in which 'the subjective' comes to givenness" (Husserl, 1910–1911/2006, p. 164).

Early formulators of EPR asked researchers to identify "central themes" in each "meaning unit" of data (Giorgi, 1975) and to organize the data "into *clusters of themes* . . . which are common to all of the subject's protocols" (Colaizzi, 1967, 1978, p. 59, italics in original; see also Van Kaam, 1966). Today, there have emerged new qualitative methods in psychology built, in part, on an identification of "themes" within interview and protocol data (e.g., Braun & Clarke, 2006). One difference, however, is that in phenomenological research, these themes are culled directly from the data, often using the participant's verbal formulations, whereas, in adaptations of thematic analysis in more recent research traditions, themes are sometimes introduced by the researchers themselves in the form of pregiven "codes" that enable research teams to "recognize" the themes in the data. In contrast, the phenomenological method with its *epoché* (bracketing) of preconceptions places the researcher's focus decisively on the words and ultimately the meanings belonging to the participants, thereby avoiding the possibility of falling into a tautology in the conduct of research, where one "discovers" in the data the very presuppositions that have been guiding the research from the start—while also avoiding "confirmation bias" in the validation of qualitative findings by other researchers.

ACHIEVING METHODOLOGICAL INTEGRITY

In their task force reports on designing and reporting qualitative research, Levitt et al. (2017, 2018) together made a major contribution to the procedural literature by drawing our attention to the many ways in which methodological "fidelity" and "integrity" should ideally guide every step of qualitative research. In Wertz's contribution to the first task force's presentation of integrity in the conduct of research, he had "intended the idea to refer to the internal compatibility of the various constituents of method, meaning the way each constituent of method was useful for the research as a whole" (F. J. Wertz, personal communication, May 3, 2020). This idea that each part of the whole of a method should serve the interest of the whole has a double significance. First, it means that each part of the method is to be "integrated" with the rest of the method, and in this sense, methodological integrity is addressed. Second, each part of the method must have a functional "utility" within the whole.

> The issue of utility has to do with relationship of all aspects of the methodology to the specific research aims; this includes not only the phenomenon researched but the questions being asked about it, which go back to the gaps in received knowledge, the deficiencies of other research, and so on. (F. J. Wertz, personal communication, May 3, 2020)

As an example of this in EPR, I referred in Chapter 6 to how in the Discussion section of a research report, there should be a return to the literature reviewed in the Introduction to assess the extent to which the current study has successfully addressed the research aims spelled out earlier. This, in turn, is related to what Heidegger (1925/1985) referred to as "what is asked for" in any inquiry: Have the results genuinely revealed what the researcher set out to understand? This would be one criterion for utility. Having the researcher enter into "dialogue" with the authors whose work was either built on or critiqued is furthermore a way that the researcher is then held "accountable" for challenges made at the outset of the study.

Beyond this, integrity would mean that all the constituents of the research—the philosophical assumptions of the research, selection of participants, the procedures of data collection, the kinds of analysis performed, and even the reporting and dissemination of findings—would all cohere together and usefully support each other in the service of the goals of the research. In some of the excerpts from research reports presented throughout this book, two student researchers (and their families) were themselves immigrants who had suffered humiliation and thereby were stakeholders in their respective research questions. My suggestion for these researchers to be collecting data in the native tongue of their informants was intended as a way of ensuring fidelity to the phenomenon by being sure that the participants would be able to express themselves without being compromised by having to speak in a language less familiar to them. Also, in terms of fidelity to the stated method, the report of the research has to cohere with regard to the aims presented in the Introduction, how the data were collected, the actual process of data analysis, and so on, for the research to have integrity. Ultimately, if the report is to be useful, it should tie together all the various procedures used in the research in a coherent way and should not merely cite the methodologies of others without spelling out how they were adapted to one's own specific interests and abilities. In summary, the various constituents of the research have to be consistent with each other and useful in their interrelations as they serve the overarching goals of the research. After all, every part of the research must ultimately serve the goals of the investigation, as well as being presented in harmony with each other.

Aspiring Toward Internal Validity

For the findings of EPR to be faithful to the experiences investigated and thereby achieve what Levitt et al. (2017) referred to as "methodological fidelity," it is important to avoid tautologies and other self-fulfilling prophecies whereby the researcher's presuppositions get in the way of letting the findings emerge directly from analysis of the data. The phenomenological *epoché* or bracketing effectively holds these presuppositions "in check," while the reduction enables researchers to experience firsthand the process of discovering their phenomenon through direct existential contact or "intuition" (*an-schauen*: "looking-at" the evidence). Merleau-Ponty (1945/1962) suggested the impossibility of a complete suspension of perspectivity (p. xiv), the latter being an essential feature of any act of consciousness. This means that we must learn and help others learn how to recognize the assumptions that guide our scientific investigations, and we must learn how to use those assumptions with great care. Gadamer (1960/1975) wrote, "All correct interpretation must be on guard against arbitrary fancies and the limitations imposed by imperceptible habits of thought and direct its gaze 'on the things themselves'" (p. 236). The employment of the phenomenological *epoché* enables the researcher to put aside their assumptions and examine the data quite literally on their own terms. This then prevents the researcher from mistaking their beliefs as scientific findings. It was precisely the bracketing of what Sartre termed "impure reflection" (a term he used to characterize formal psychological theorizing as well as everyday self-deception) that enabled him to engage in the "purifying reflection" that brought him more faithfully to the encounter with his subject matter—one that he believed to be impervious to the linear determinisms expressed by "natural science" psychology. This is just one of the ways that EPR achieves what Levitt et al. (2017) referred to as methodological "fidelity."

Aspiring Toward External Validity

Although one rarely hears qualitative researchers talking about the "external validity" of their findings (for the simple reason that qualitative researchers typically only make knowledge claims with reference to the sample that was actually studied), it turns out to be one of the distinguishing characteristics of EPR (with its foundation in Husserl's method of "free variation in the imagination") that enables it to make knowledge claims that, in principle, can reach "beyond the sample to the population"—or, expressed phenomenologically, beyond the individual experience to the "universe of possible instances" of the phenomenon (Husserl, 1925/1977, pp. 53–65).

The movement from individual to general levels of analysis is not simply a matter of looking for commonalities among the individual cases that were studied empirically. It is, rather, a procedure that enables the researcher to transcend the limitations of the instances used as a point of departure for reflection (Churchill, 2006, pp. 90–93; Husserl, 1948/1973, pp. 340–344; Wertz, 2010). As described in Chapter 5, our move to the general level is accomplished by mentally running through a plurality of instances, both empirically given (in the form of participants' experiences) and imaginatively conjured (via "free variation in fantasy") until a "unity of sense" becomes apparent with regard to the "world of experience" portrayed in the instances. This unity represents for Husserl (1948/1973) a "nucleus of meaning" that remains explicitly given through all of the variations displayed to the researcher's consciousness, whether in reading data or envisioning alternative scenarios in the mind's eye—all of which constitute the evidence (*Evidenz*) to which Husserl enjoined us to "bring ourselves" (in his earlier quoted "battle cry"):

> The essence proves to be that without which an object of a particular kind cannot be thought, that is, without which the object cannot be intuitively imagined as such. . . . the variants here and there are, in like fashion, *arbitrary particularizations of the one eidos*. (p. 341, italics in original)

In other words, "free" variation allows for "arbitrary" sampling from the universe of possible experiences in the researcher's imagination. Without using this procedure of free variation, the researcher can only articulate results that have a claim to validity relative to the experiences actually studied but not to the entire universe of such experiences.

Finding commonality among five, 50, even 500 examples is still only a finite empirical commonality. It may be a step in the direction of "general knowledge claims," but it cannot make the claim of universality that the phenomenologist who practices eidetic intuition can make. A genuinely phenomenological structural description would be distilled down to only what is essential—that is, to those characteristics that have to exist in every imaginable case. Therefore, any characteristics that are there in some cases— even if representing all of the sample—but not in every imaginable case would not then qualify as general phenomenological findings. Each sentence of a phenomenological structure needs to characterize every empirical or imagined instance where the phenomenon is given as evidence.

In the end, what is truly "phenomenological" about the kind of research described here is not simply its foundation in individual experience— because the latter would characterize any human science research conducted from within what Husserl (1930/1970) called the "personal attitude" (p. 317). Rather, the distinguishing characteristic of the classical phenomenological method lies in the researcher's movement from individual to universal possibilities of experience by means of this reflective procedure of free variation. Indeed, it is the arbitrariness or randomness of the variations produced in the researcher's imagination that ensures the generalizability of the study, just as it is the randomness of sampling in experimental research that ensures the "external validity" of results. Unfortunately, researchers do not typically write down the random variations produced in their mind's eye; otherwise, I could include examples. Only the final results of this procedure get published as the "general structural descriptions" (GSD), which can then be subjected to the reader's "verification." Indeed, if the reader can think of any example of the phenomenon under investigation that cannot be characterized by the GSD, then the findings would be invalid—that is, they would be unfaithful to the universe of possible experiences. The reader might return to the example of a GSD in Chapter 5 for the experience of being-anxious and ask themself, "Can I think of any instance of anxiety where this would not be the case?" The same challenge could be made in rereading the GSD for immigrant humiliation, also cited in Chapter 5, except that there, the researcher was careful not to make a knowledge claim for her GSD, which she presented in her Discussion rather than in her Results. Given her limited data and her newness to the practice of EPR, she more humbly entitled this part of her thesis "Towards a General Structural Description" and thus open to further reflection and revision.

STRENGTHS, LIMITATIONS, AND FUTURE DIRECTIONS

Strengths and Advantages of EPR

If one wants simply to enumerate the diverse ways something is experienced, perhaps a simple form of thematic analysis is sufficient, but if one aims at higher levels of generality and wants to know the interrelations of the various constituents of the phenomenon, then structural analysis is needed for the research to have integrity. The emphasis of the EPR paradigm can be described as a "fidelity toward the phenomenon," where a psychological phenomenon is understood not as an event "in itself" but rather as something that occurs "for someone." Situations in which we experience anger, jealousy, joy, futility, intimacy, courage, self-esteem, self-deception, being victimized, and so on, are not approached by the EP researcher as though there were some objective reference point from which to observe and describe the events taking place. Rather, there is an acknowledgment of an "always already" existing perspective through which the individual experiences their world and, in turn, through which the researcher takes up the experience of the individual.

The chief virtue of EPR lies in its capacity for rendering clear, concrete, and comprehensible articulations of experiences that heretofore have been dismissed as "subjective" and thereby "private" and "inaccessible" to empirical analysis.

Limitations and Weaknesses of EPR

The greatest struggle involved in this tradition of research probably lies in its final stage—namely, the description of one's findings. This is not to say that the earlier stages of intuition and analysis do not present the researcher with enormous challenges, especially when the experiences under investigation do not originate in one's own experience but in the experience of others. The limitations of the method come to bear in the researcher's ability to articulate their findings. In the final pages of my dissertation, I wrote,

> The limits of my findings ultimately reflect the limits of my vision. . . . If I am not satisfied with my findings, it is because I know that there was more to be seen. What I was capable of seeing, I wrote down as findings. But there was also an opacity of the data that I was unable to penetrate. The limits of my vision can be found in the findings themselves. My blind spots are evident wherever I have failed to achieve a truly structural articulation of the phenomenon. (Churchill, 1984, pp. 215–216)

It is because of the limitations of our vision that immersing ourselves in the primary and secondary source phenomenological literature is important on one's path to becoming an EP researcher. As primatologist Frans de Waal (2001) observed in *The Ape and the Sushi Master*, we learn how to do difficult things through observation. It takes some practice to learn how to produce the kind of findings that might bear the character of an aspiring "EPR master." And yet, one can see in the examples from undergraduate research projects used throughout this book that it is possible even for beginners to produce insightful and valuable results.

This method will be of no use to those who wish to gain explanatory (cause-and-effect) knowledge about their psychological phenomena. You will not be able to state with any confidence what "the effect" of any given set of circumstances would be on the average person if you are using EPR. Such questions must be left for those equipped with experimental procedures, with their corresponding descriptive and inferential statistical methods.

One of the critical concerns with the application of phenomenology to the field of qualitative research is that while more researchers are calling their work phenomenological, it seems that only a small percentage of contemporary qualitative studies bear a faithful relationship to the guiding principles of phenomenology (for good anthologies, see C. T. Fischer, 2006; Giorgi et al., 1971, 1975, 1979, 1983; Pollio et al., 1998; Valle, 1998; Valle & Halling, 1989). The problem here stems from the fact that many researchers consider their research to be "phenomenological" simply because their data consist of first-person reports or testimonies. I can attest to this as a journal editor who receives submissions of such research from around the world.

The problem is that these studies referring to themselves as "phenomeno-logical" on the basis of their self-report data alone can cause confusion among students seeking to learn the method because these studies stop short of a genuine "intentional analysis," stop short of arriving at essences, and stop short of a structural interweaving of essential thematic findings. There should not be a cafeteria approach to phenomenology, where you just take what you want from the method and leave the rest behind. The bottom line here is Heidegger's (1927/1962, p. 59) remark cited earlier about the term *phenomenology* defining the "how" (the method of analysis) and not the "what" (the data) of the research.

Future Directions

The future of phenomenological psychology will entirely depend on researchers' interest and willingness to be guided back to the "matters themselves" to be discovered in intentionality and to engage themselves steadfastly with the primary source texts within the field, which are often challenging and difficult yet infinitely rewarding if one is ready and willing to go to the encounter.

In addressing ourselves to questions of global importance, we recover the purpose and significance of our work as scientists and at the same time remember our belonging to a wider scientific, academic, and human commu-nity. It is the relevance of science to human affairs that ultimately connects the various sciences and provides a basis for dialogue among researchers. Research findings are then addressed to the scientific community at large, and researchers at all levels are able to enter into collaborative dialogue with each other. "Accordingly, genuinely human research, into any phenom-enon whatsoever, by seriously including the trusting dialogal approach, passes beyond research in its limited sense and occasions existential insight" (Colaizzi, 1978, p. 69).

In the end, the value of our research investigations—and our research traditions—will depend on their ability to help us to gain insight into the vicissitudes of human experience. Beyond what we and our participants gain from our research together, there is further gain on the part of our readers who are able to enter into and appreciate our work. Existential phenomeno-logical research thus enables researchers to enter into the experiences of their research participants, just as it invites readers to enter into not only the experiences investigated but also the experience itself of doing psychology phenomenologically.

Appendix

EXEMPLAR STUDIES (1971-2020)

Aanstoos, C. M. (1985). The structure of thinking in chess. In A. Giorgi (Ed.), *Phenomenology and psychological research* (pp. 86–117). Duquesne University Press.

Alapack, R. J. (1975). The outlaw relationship: An existential phenomenological reflection. In A. Giorgi, C. T. Fischer, & E. L. Murray (Eds.), *Duquesne studies in phenomenological psychology* (Vol. 2, pp. 182–205). Duquesne University Press. https://doi.org/10.5840/dspp1975215

Beck, T. (2013). A phenomenological analysis of anxiety as experienced in social situations. *Journal of Phenomenological Psychology, 44*(2), 179–219. https://doi.org/10.1163/15691624-12341255

Churchill, S. D., Lowery, J., McNally, O., & Rao, A. (1998). The question of reliability in interpretive psychological research: A comparison of three phenomenologically-based protocol analyses. In R. Valle (Ed.), *Phenomenological inquiry: Existential and transpersonal dimensions* (pp. 63–85). Plenum Press. https://doi.org/10.1007/978-1-4899-0125-5_3

DeRobertis, E. M. & Bland, A. M. (2020). From personal threat to cross-cultural learning: An eidetic investigation. *Journal of Phenomenological Psychology, 51*(1), 1–15. https://doi.org/10.1163/15691624-12341368

Englander, M. (2007). Persistent psychological meaning of early emotional memories. *Journal of Phenomenological Psychology, 38*(2), 181–216. https://doi.org/10.1163/156916207X234275

Fischer, C. T. (1998). Being angry revealed as self-deceptive protest: An empirical phenomenological analysis. In R. Valle (Ed.), *Phenomenological inquiry: Existential and transpersonal perspectives* (pp. 111–122). Plenum Press. https://doi.org/10.1007/978-1-4899-0125-5_5

Fischer, W. F. (1974). On the phenomenological mode of researching "being anxious." *Journal of Phenomenological Psychology, 4*(2), 405–423. https://doi.org/10.1163/156916274X00045

Fischer, W. F. (1985). Self-deception: An existential-phenomenological investigation into its essential meanings. In A. Giorgi (Ed.), *Phenomenology and psychological research* (pp. 118–154). Duquesne University Press.

Giorgi, A. (1975). An application of phenomenological method in psychology. In A. Giorgi, C. Fischer, & E. Murray (Eds.), *Duquesne studies in phenomenological psychology* (Vol. 2, pp. 82–103). Duquesne University Press. https://doi.org/10.5840/dspp197529

Morley, J. (1998). The private theater: A phenomenological investigation of daydreaming. *Journal of Phenomenological Psychology, 29*(1), 116–134. https://doi.org/10.1163/156916298X00049

Moss, D. (1982). Distortions in human embodiment: A study of surgically treated obesity. In R. Bruzina & B. Wilshire (Eds.), *Selected studies in phenomenology and existential philosophy: Vol. 8. Phenomenology, dialogues and bridges* (pp. 253–267). State University of New York.

Rao, A. & Churchill, S. D. (2004). Experiencing oneself as being beautiful: A phenomenological study informed by Sartre's ontology. *Qualitative Research in Psychology, 1*(1), 55–68.

Robinson, F. A. (1998). Dissociative women's experiences of self-cutting. In R. Valle (Ed.), *Phenomenological inquiry: Existential and transpersonal perspectives* (pp. 209–225). Plenum Press. https://doi.org/10.1007/978-1-4899-0125-5_9

Robinson, P., Giorgi, B., & Ekman, S.-L. (2012). The lived experience of early-stage Alzheimer's disease: A three-year longitudinal phenomenological case study. *Journal of Phenomenological Psychology, 43*(2), 216–238. https://doi.org/10.1163/15691624-12341236

Røseth, I., Binder, P.-E., & Malt, U. F. (2013). Engulfed by an alienated and threatening emotional body: The essential meaning structure of depression in women. *Journal of Phenomenological Psychology, 44*(2), 153–178. https://doi.org/10.1163/15691624-12341254

Shertock, T. (1998). Latin American women's experience of feeling able to move toward and accomplish a meaningful and challenging goal. In R. Valle (Ed.), *Phenomenological inquiry: Existential and transpersonal perspectives* (pp. 157–174). Plenum Press. https://doi.org/10.1007/978-1-4899-0125-5_7

Stevick, E. (1971). An empirical investigation of the experience of anger. In A. Giorgi, W. F. Fischer, & R. von Eckartsberg (Eds.), *Duquesne studies in phenomenological psychology* (Vol. 1, pp. 132–148). Duquesne University Press. https://doi.org/10.5840/dspp1971114

Wertz, F. J. (1985). Methods and findings in an empirical analysis of "being criminally victimized." In A. Giorgi (Ed.), *Phenomenology and psychological research* (pp. 155–216). Duquesne University Press.

Zapien, N. (2016). The beginning of an extra-marital affair: A descriptive phenomenological psychological study and clinical implications. *Journal of Phenomenological Psychology, 47*(2), 134–155. https://doi.org/10.1163/15691624-12341311

References

Aanstoos, C. M. (1985). The structure of thinking in chess. In A. Giorgi (Ed.), *Phenomenology and psychological research* (pp. 86–117). Duquesne University Press.

Adams, W. W. (2016). Ecopsychology by way of phenomenology. In C. T. Fischer, R. Brooke, & L. Laubscher (Eds.), *The qualitative vision for psychology: An invitation to a human science approach* (pp. 221–243). Duquesne University Press.

American Psychological Association. (2020). *Publication manual of the American Psychological Association* (7th ed.). https://doi.org/10.1037/0000165-000

Angel, S. (2013). Grasping the experience of the other from an interview: Self-transposition in use. *International Journal of Qualitative Studies on Health and Well-being, 8*(1), Article 20634. https://doi.org/10.3402/qhw.v8i0.20634

Applebaum, M. (2014). Intentionality and narrativity in phenomenological psychological research: Reflections on Husserl and Ricoeur. *Indo-Pacific Journal of Phenomenology, 14*(2), 1–19. https://doi.org/10.2989/IPJP.2014.14.2.2.1241

Ashworth, P. (2003). An approach to phenomenological psychology: The contingencies of the lifeworld. *Journal of Phenomenological Psychology, 34*(2), 145–156. https://doi.org/10.1163/156916203322847119

Beck, C. T. (2021). *Introduction to phenomenology: Focus on methodology*. SAGE.

Berger, P. L., & Luckmann, T. (1966). *The social construction of reality: A treatise on the sociology of knowledge*. Doubleday.

Braun, V., & Clarke, V. (2006). Using thematic analysis in psychology. *Qualitative Research in Psychology, 3*(2), 77–101. https://doi.org/10.1191/1478088706qp063oa

Brentano, F. (1973). *Psychology from an empirical standpoint* (A. C. Rancurello, D. B. Terrell, & L. L. McAlister, Trans.). Humanities Press. (Original work published 1874)

Churchill, S. D. (1984). *Psychodiagnostic seeing: A phenomenological investigation of the psychologist's experience during the interview phase of a clinical assessment* [Doctoral dissertation, Duquesne University]. Dissertation Abstracts International.

Churchill, S. D. (1990). Considerations for teaching a phenomenological approach to psychological research. *Journal of Phenomenological Psychology, 21*(1), 46–67. https://doi.org/10.1163/156916290X00119

Churchill, S. D. (1991). Reasons, causes, and motives: Psychology's illusive explanations of behavior. *Theoretical and Philosophical Psychology, 11*(1), 24–34. https://doi.org/10.1037/h0091504

Churchill, S. D. (1998). The intentionality of psychodiagnostic seeing: A phenomenological investigation of clinical impression formation. In R. Valle (Ed.), *Phenomenological inquiry: Existential and transpersonal dimensions* (pp. 175–207). Plenum Press. https://doi.org/10.1007/978-1-4899-0125-5_8

Churchill, S. D. (2000). Seeing through self-deception in verbal reports: Finding methodological virtue in problematic data. *Journal of Phenomenological Psychology, 31*(1), 44–62. https://doi.org/10.1163/156916200746247

Churchill, S. D. (2006). Phenomenological analysis: Impression formation during a clinical assessment interview. In C. T. Fischer (Ed.), *Qualitative research methods for psychologists: Introduction through empirical studies* (pp. 79–110). Academic Press. https://doi.org/10.1016/B978-012088470-4/50007-7

Churchill, S. D. (2010a). Methodological considerations for human science research in the wake of postmodernism: Remembering our ground while envisioning our future. In M. Tarozzi (Ed.), *Phenomenology and human science today: Thoughts and research* (pp. 155–178). Zeta Books.

Churchill, S. D. (2010b). "Second person" perspectivity in observing and understanding emotional expression. In L. Embree, M. Barber, & T. Nenon (Eds.), *Phenomenology 2010. Vol. 5: Selected essays from North America. Part 2: Phenomenology beyond philosophy* (pp. 81–106). Zeta Books/Arghos-Diffusion.

Churchill, S. D. (2012). Teaching phenomenology by way of "second-person perspectivity." *Indo-Pacific Journal of Phenomenology, 12.* http://www.ipjp.org/component/jdownloads/send/11-the-teaching-of-phenomenology-september-2012/207-teaching-phenomenology-by-way-of-second-person-perspectivity-from-my-thirty-years-at-the-university-of-dallas-by-scott-d-churchill

Churchill, S. D. (2013). Heideggerian pathways through trauma and recovery: A "hermeneutics of facticity." *The Humanistic Psychologist, 41*(3), 219–230. https://doi.org/10.1080/08873267.2013.800768

Churchill, S. D. (2014). Phenomenology. In T. Teo (Ed.), *Encyclopedia of critical psychology* (pp. 1389–1402). Elsevier. https://doi.org/10.1007/978-1-4614-5583-7_219

Churchill, S. D. (2016). Resonating with meaning in the lives of others: Invitation to empathic understanding. In C. T. Fischer, R. Brooke, & L. Laubscher (Eds.), *The qualitative vision for psychology: An invitation to a human science approach* (pp. 91–116). Duquesne University Press.

Churchill, S. D. (2018a). On the empathic mode of intuition: A phenomenological foundation for social psychiatry. In M. Englander (Ed.), *Phenomenology and the social context of psychiatry* (pp. 65–93). Bloomsbury.

Churchill, S. D. (2018b). Explorations in teaching the phenomenological method: Challenging students to "grasp at meaning" in human science research. *Qualitative Psychology, 5*(2), 207–227. https://doi.org/10.1037/qup0000116

Churchill, S. D., Lowery, J., McNally, O., & Rao, A. (1998). The question of reliability in interpretive psychological research: A comparison of three phenomenologically-based protocol analyses. In R. Valle (Ed.), *Phenomenological inquiry: Existential and transpersonal dimensions* (pp. 63–85). Plenum Press. https://doi.org/10.1007/978-1-4899-0125-5_3

Churchill, S. D., & Wertz, F. J. (1985). An introduction to phenomenological psychology for consumer research. In E. C. Hirschman & M. B. Holbrook (Eds.), *Advances in consumer research* (Vol. 12, pp. 550–555). Association for Consumer Research.

Churchill, S. D., & Wertz, F. J. (2015). An introduction to phenomenological research in psychology: Historical, conceptual, and methodological foundations. In K. Schneider, J. F. T. Bugental, & J. F. Pierson (Eds.), *The handbook of humanistic psychology* (Rev. ed., pp. 275–295). SAGE.

Colaizzi, P. F. (1967). Analysis of the learner's perception of learning material at various phases of a learning process. *Review of Existential Psychology & Psychiatry, 7,* 95–105. https://doi.org/10.5840/dspp1971112

Colaizzi, P. F. (1973). *Reflection and research in psychology.* Kendall/Hunt.

Colaizzi, P. F. (1978). Psychological research as the phenomenologist views it. In R. S. Valle & M. King (Eds.), *Existential-phenomenological alternatives for psychology* (pp. 48–71). Oxford University Press.

Colaizzi, P. F. (2001). A note on "fundamental structures" thirty years later. *Methods: A Journal for Human Science, 16,* 7–10.

Colaizzi, P. F. (2002). Kant and the problem of "intuition": An essay on the misinterpretations of Kant's philosophy in particular and of philosophy in general. *Methods: A Journal for Human Science, 17,* 7–47.

Dahlberg, K., Dahlberg, H., & Nyström, M. (2008). *Reflective lifeworld research* (2nd ed.). Studentlitteratur AB.

Davidson, L., & Cosgrove, L. A. (2003). Psychologism and phenomenological psychology revisited (Part II): The return to positivity. *Journal of Phenomenological Psychology, 33*(2), 141–177.

de Beauvoir, S. (2010). *The second sex* (C. Borde & S. Malovany-Chevallier, Trans.). Alfred A. Knopf. (Original work published 1949)

DeRobertis, E. (2017). *The phenomenology of learning and becoming: Enthusiasm, creativity, and self-development.* Palgrave. https://doi.org/10.1057/978-1-349-95204-5

de Waal, F. (2001). *The ape and the sushi master: Cultural reflections of a primatologist.* Basic Books.

Dilthey, W. (1977a). Ideas concerning a descriptive and analytic psychology. In *Descriptive psychology and historical understanding* (pp. 21–120) (R. M. Zaner, Trans.). Martinus Nijhoff. (Original work written 1894 and published 1924) https://doi.org/10.1007/978-94-009-9658-8_2

Dilthey, W. (1977b). The understanding of other persons and their expressions of life. In *Descriptive psychology and historical understanding* (pp. 121–144) (K. L. Heiges, Trans.). Martinus Nijhoff. (Original work published 1927) https://doi.org/10.1007/978-94-009-9658-8_3

Englander, M. (2016). The phenomenological method in qualitative psychology and psychiatry. *International Journal of Qualitative Studies on Health and Well-Being, 11*(1), Article 30682. https://doi.org/10.3402/qhw.v11.30682

Englander, M. (2018). Empathy in a social psychiatry. In M. Englander (Ed.), *Phenomenology and the social context of psychiatry: Social relations, psychopathology, and Husserl's philosophy* (pp. 49–64). Bloomsbury Academic.

Englander, M. (2019). General knowledge claims in qualitative research. *The Humanistic Psychologist, 47*(1), 1–14. https://doi.org/10.1037/hum0000107

Englander, M. (2020). Phenomenological psychological interviewing. *The Humanistic Psychologist, 48*(1), 54–73. https://doi.org/10.1037/hum0000144

Finlay, L. (2003). The reflexive journey: Mapping multiple routes. In L. Finlay & B. Gough (Eds.), *Reflexivity: A practical guide for researchers in health and social sciences* (pp. 3–20). Wiley-Blackwell.

Finlay, L. (2011). *Phenomenology for therapists: Researching the lived world.* Wiley-Blackwell. https://doi.org/10.1002/9781119975144

Finlay, L. (Ed.). (2017). Reflexivity [Special issue]. *Qualitative Psychology, 3*(2), 119–198.

Fischer, C. T. (1994). Rigor in qualitative research: Reflexive and presentational. *Methods: A Journal for Human Science, 9*, 21–27.

Fischer, C. T. (1998). Being angry revealed as self-deceptive protest: An empirical phenomenological analysis. In R. Valle (Ed.), *Phenomenological inquiry: Existential and transpersonal perspectives* (pp. 111–122). Plenum Press. https://doi.org/10.1007/978-1-4899-0125-5_5

Fischer, C. T. (Ed.). (2006). *Qualitative research methods for psychologists: Introduction through empirical studies*. Academic Press.

Fischer, W. F. (1974). On the phenomenological mode of researching "being anxious." *Journal of Phenomenological Psychology, 4*(2), 405–423. https://doi.org/10.1163/156916274X00045

Fischer, W. F. (1978). An empirical-phenomenological investigation of being-anxious: An example of the meanings of being-emotional. In R. S. Valle & M. King (Eds.), *Existential-phenomenological alternatives for psychology* (pp. 166–181). Oxford University Press.

Fischer, W. F. (1985). Self-deception: An existential-phenomenological investigation into its essential meanings. In A. Giorgi (Ed.), *Phenomenology and psychological research* (pp. 118–154). Duquesne University Press.

Freud, S. (1963). *Dora: An analysis of a case of hysteria.* Collier. (Original work published 1905)

Frankl, V. (1959). *Man's search for meaning.* Washington Square Press.

Gadamer, H. G. (1975). *Truth and method* (G. Barden & J. Cumming, Eds. & Trans.). Crossroad. (Original work published 1960)

Galvin, K., & Todres, L. (2013). *Caring and well-being: A lifeworld approach.* Routledge. https://doi.org/10.4324/9780203082898

Gannt, E. E., & Williams, R. N. (2016). Explanation versus understanding in psychology: A human science approach. In C. T. Fischer, R. Brooke, & L. Laubscher (Eds.), *The qualitative vision for psychology: An invitation to a human science approach* (pp. 31–48). Duquesne University Press.

Garza, G. (2004). Thematic moment analysis: A didactic application of a procedure for phenomenological analysis of narrative data. *The Humanistic Psychologist, 32*(2), 120–168. https://doi.org/10.1080/08873267.2004.9961749

Garza, G. (2007). Varieties of phenomenological research at the University of Dallas: An emerging typology. *Qualitative Research in Psychology, 4*(4), 313–342. https://doi.org/10.1080/14780880701551170

Gendlin, E. (1978). *Focusing.* Everest House.

Giorgi, A. (1970). *Psychology as a human science: A phenomenologically based approach.* Harper & Row.

Giorgi, A. (1975). An application of phenomenological method in psychology. In A. Giorgi, C. Fischer, & E. Murray (Eds.), *Duquesne studies in phenomenological psychology* (Vol. II, pp. 82–103). Duquesne University Press. https://doi.org/10.5840/dspp197529

Giorgi, A. (1985). Sketch of a psychological phenomenological method. In A. Giorgi (Ed.), *Phenomenology and psychological research* (pp. 8–22). Duquesne University Press.

Giorgi, A. (2009). *The descriptive phenomenological method in psychology: A modified Husserlian approach.* Duquesne University Press.

Giorgi, A. (2014). Phenomenological philosophy as the basis for a human scientific psychology. *The Humanistic Psychologist, 42*(3), 233–248. https://doi.org/10.1080/08873267.2014.933052

Giorgi, A., Barton, A., & Maes, C. (Eds.). (1983). *Duquesne studies in phenomenological psychology: Volume IV.* Duquesne University Press.

Giorgi, A., Fischer, C., & Murray, E. (Eds.). (1975). *Duquesne studies in phenomenological psychology: Volume II.* Duquesne University Press.

Giorgi, A., Fischer, W., & von Eckartsberg, R. (Eds.). (1971). *Duquesne studies in phenomenological psychology: Volume I.* Duquesne University Press.

Giorgi, A., Knowles, R., & Smith, D. L. (Eds.). (1979). *Duquesne studies in phenomenological psychology: Volume III.* Duquesne University Press.

Gosline, N. (2016). *Finding a way out: A phenomenological study of women who have left domestic violence situations and their courage for creating a life of their own* [Unpublished senior thesis]. University of Dallas.

Gurwitsch, A. (1974). *Phenomenology and the theory of science* (L. Embree, Ed.). Northwestern University Press.

Gurwitsch, A. (1979). *Human encounters in the social world* (A. Métraux, Ed.; F. Kersten, Trans.). Duquesne University Press. (Original work published 1977)

Halling, S. (2008). *Intimacy, transcendence, and psychology: Closeness and openness in everyday life.* Palgrave.

Halling, S., Kunz, G., & Rowe, J. O. (1994). The contributions of dialogal psychology to phenomenological research. *Journal of Humanistic Psychology*, *34*(1), 109–131. https://doi.org/10.1177/00221678940341007

Halling, S., Leifer, M., & Rowe, J. (2006). The emergence of the dialogal approach: Forgiving another. In C. T. Fischer (Ed.), *Qualitative research methods for psychologists: Introduction through empirical studies* (pp. 247–277). Academic Press. https://doi.org/10.1016/B978-012088470-4/50012-0

Heidegger, M. (1962). *Being and time* (J. MacQuarrie & E. Robinson, Trans.). Harper & Row. (Original work published 1927)

Heidegger, M. (1985). *History of the concept of time: Prolegomena* (T. Kisiel, Trans.). Indiana University Press. (Original lecture course given 1925)

Heidegger, M. (1999). *Ontology: The hermeneutics of facticity* (J. van Buren, Trans.). Indiana University Press. (Original lecture course presented 1923 and published 1988)

Heidegger, M. (2011). *The concept of time: The first draft of* Being and Time (I. Farin & A Skinner, Trans.). Continuum. (Original lecture course presented 1924 and published 2004)

Husserl, E. (1962). *Ideas: General introduction to pure phenomenology* (W. R. B. Gibson, Trans.). Collier Books. (Original work published 1913)

Husserl, E. (1968). *Logische Untersuchungen: Zweiter Band: Untersuchungen zur Phänomenologie und Theorie der Erkenntnis—I. Teil* [Logical investigations: Vol. 2. Investigations in phenomenology and the theory of knowledge—Part 1] (5th ed.). Max Niemeyer Verlag. (Original work published 1901)

Husserl, E. (1970). The attitude of natural science and the attitude of humanistic science (W. Biemel, Ed.). In E. Husserl, *The crisis of European sciences and transcendental phenomenology* (D. Carr, Trans.; pp. 315–334), Northwestern University Press. (Original work drafted 1930 and published 1954)

Husserl, E. (1973). *Experience and judgment* (J. S. Churchill and J. Ameriks, Trans.). Northwestern University Press. (Original work published 1948)

Husserl, E. (1977). *Phenomenological psychology: Lectures, summer semester, 1925* (J. Scanlon, Trans.). Martinus Nijhoff. (Original manuscript written in 1925 and published in 1962)

Husserl, E. (1989). *Ideas pertaining to a pure phenomenology and a phenomenological philosophy. Second book: Studies in the phenomenology of constitution* (R. Rojcewicz & A. Schuwer, Trans.). Kluwer. (Original work written 1928 and published 1952)

Husserl, E. (2006). *The basic problems of phenomenology: From the lectures, winter semester, 1910–1911* (I. Farin & J. G. Hart, Trans.). Springer.

Keen, E. (1975). *A primer in phenomenological psychology*. Holt, Rinehart, & Winston.

Keen, E. (2003). Doing psychology phenomenologically: Methodological considerations. *The Humanistic Psychologist*, *31*(4), 5–33. https://doi.org/10.1080/08873267.2003.9986932

Keen, E. (2011). Emotional narratives: Depression as sadness—anxiety as fear. *The Humanistic Psychologist, 39*(1), 66–70. https://doi.org/10.1080/08873267.2011.539937

Keen, E. (2012). Keeping the psyche in psychology. *The Humanistic Psychologist, 40*(3), 224–231. https://doi.org/10.1080/08873267.2012.642218

Koch, S., & Leary, D. E. (1985). *A century of psychology as science.* McGraw-Hill.

Kruger, D. (1979). *An introduction to phenomenological psychology.* Duquesne University Press.

Laing, R. D. (1967). *The politics of experience.* Ballantine.

Langdridge, D. (2007). *Phenomenological psychology: Theory, research, method.* Pearson.

Lee, W.-L. (2016). Phenomenology as a method for indigenous psychology. In C. T. Fischer, R. Brooke, & L. Laubscher (Eds.), *The qualitative vision for psychology: An invitation to a human science approach* (pp. 221–243). Duquesne University Press.

Levitt, H. M., Bamberg, M., Creswell, J. W., Frost, D., Josselson, R., & Suárez-Orozco, C. (2018). Journal article reporting standards for qualitative primary, qualitative meta-analytic, and mixed methods research in psychology: The APA Publications and Communications Board Task Force report. *American Psychologist, 73*(1), 26–46. https://doi.org/10.1037/amp0000151

Levitt, H. M., Motulsky, S. L., Wertz, F. J., Morrow, S. L., & Ponterotto, J. G. (2017). Recommendations for designing and reviewing qualitative research in psychology: Promoting methodological integrity. *Qualitative Psychology, 4*(1), 2–22. https://doi.org/10.1037/qup0000082

Lipps, T. (1903). *Leitfaden der Psychologie* [Textbook of psychology]. Engelmann.

Mena Ibarra, G. J. (2016). *Understanding one's adversities as meaningful sacrifices: A phenomenological inquiry into the humiliation of undocumented immigrants* [Unpublished senior thesis]. University of Dallas.

Merleau-Ponty, M. (1962). *Phenomenology of perception* (C. Smith, Trans.). Routledge. (Original work published 1945)

Merleau-Ponty, M. (1969). Preface to Hesnard's *L'oeuvre de Freud.* In A. L. Fischer (Ed.), *The essential writings of Merleau-Ponty* (A. L. Fischer, Trans.; pp. 81–87). Harcourt, Brace & World. (Original work published 1960)

Miranda, N. (2016). *Meaning-making in miscarriage: A phenomenological inquiry into the experience of coming to terms* [Unpublished senior thesis]. University of Dallas.

Morgan, A. L. (2011). *Investigating our experience in the world: A primer on qualitative inquiry.* University of Tennessee Press.

Morley, J. (1998). The private theater: A phenomenological investigation of daydreaming. *Journal of Phenomenological Psychology, 29*(1), 116–134. https://doi.org/10.1163/156916298X00049

Morley, J. (2010). It's always about the epoché: On phenomenological methodology. In T. Cloonan (Ed.), *The redirection of psychology: Essays in honor of Amedeo Giorgi* (pp. 223–232). University of Quebec Press.

Morrissey, M. B. Q. (2014). *Suffering narratives of older adults: A phenomenological study of serious illness, chronic pain, recovery, and maternal care.* Routledge. https://doi.org/10.4324/9780203741887

Moss, D. (1982). Distortions in human embodiment: A study of surgically treated obesity. In R. Bruzina & B. Wilshire (Eds.), *Selected studies in phenomenology and existential philosophy: Vol. 8. Phenomenology, dialogues and bridges* (pp. 253–267). State University of New York.

Moustakas, C. (1990). *Heuristic research: Design, methodology, and applications.* SAGE.

Moustakas, C. (1994). *Phenomenological research methods.* SAGE.

Mruk, C. J. (2010). Integrated description: A qualitative method for an evidence-based world. *The Humanistic Psychologist, 38*(4), 305–316. https://doi.org/10.1080/08873267.2010.519976

Mruk, C. (2013). *Self-esteem and positive psychology: Research, theory, and practice* (4th ed.). Springer.

Natanson, M. (1973). *Edmund Husserl: Philosopher of infinite tasks.* Northwestern University.

Nichols, B. (1981). *Ideology and the image: Social representation in the cinema and other media.* Indiana University Press.

Packer, M. J. (2017). *The science of qualitative research* (2nd ed.). Cambridge University Press. https://doi.org/10.1017/9781108264907

Palinkas, L. A., Horwitz, S. M., Green, C. A., Wisdom, J. P., Duan, N., & Hoagwood, K. (2015). Purposeful sampling for qualitative data collection and analysis in mixed method implementation research. *Administration and Policy in Mental Health, 42*(5), 533–544. https://doi.org/10.1007/s10488-013-0528-y

Plantinga, C. (1999). The scene of empathy and the human face on film. In C. Plantinga & G. M. Smith (Eds.), *Passionate views: Film, cognition, and emotion* (pp. 239–255). Johns Hopkins University Press.

Pollio, H. R., Henley, T., & Thompson, C. B. (1998). *The phenomenology of everyday life.* Cambridge University Press.

Rao, A., & Churchill, S. D. (2004). Experiencing oneself as being beautiful: A phenomenological study informed by Sartre's ontology. *Qualitative Research in Psychology, 1*(1), 55–68.

Reik, T. (1948). *Listening with the third ear: The inner experience of a psychoanalyst.* Farrar, Straus, and Giroux.

Romanyshyn, R. D. (2007). *The wounded researcher: Research with soul in mind.* Spring Books.

Ross, H. (Director). (1972). *Play it again, Sam.* Paramount Pictures.

Ruiz de Somocurcio, D. (2016). *A phenomenological approach to self-esteem and the view of the future through the eyes of an undocumented Latino immigrant brought by his/her parents to the United States as a child* [Unpublished senior thesis]. University of Dallas.

Salner, M. (1996). Researcher self-reflexivity, illusion and self-deception in qualitative research. *Methods: A Journal for Human Science, 11*, 3–27.

Sartre, J.-P. (1948). *The emotions: Outline for a theory* (B. Frechtman, Trans.). Philosophical Library. (Original work published 1939)

Sartre, J.-P. (1956). *Being and nothingness: An essay on phenomenological ontology* (H. Barnes, Trans.). Philosophical Library. (Original work published 1943)

Sartre, J.-P. (1963). *Saint Genet: Actor and martyr*. New American Library. (Original work published 1952)

Schütz, A. (1962). *Collected papers. I: The problem of social reality* (M. Natanson, Ed.). Martinus Nijhoff.

Schütz, A. (1967). *The phenomenology of the social world* (G. Walsh & F. Lehnert, Trans.). Northwestern University Press. (Original work published 1932)

Schütz, A. (1970). *On phenomenology and social relations: Selected writings* (H. R. Wagner, Ed.). The University of Chicago Press.

Schütz, A., & Luckmann, T. (1973). *The structures of the life-world* (R. Zaner & H. T. Engelhardt, Jr., Trans.). Northwestern University Press.

Shapiro, K. J. (1985). *Bodily reflective modes: A phenomenological method for psychology*. Duke University Press.

Smith, J., Flowers, P., & Larken, M. (2009). *Interpretative phenomenological analysis: Theory, method, and research*. SAGE.

Spiegelberg, H. (1975). *Doing phenomenology: Essays in and on phenomenology*. Martinus Nihjoff. https://doi.org/10.1007/978-94-010-1670-4

Spiegelberg, H. (1982). *The phenomenological movement* (3rd ed.). Martinus Nihjoff.

Stein, E. (1989). *The collected works of Edith Stein: Vol. 3. On the problem of empathy* (W. Stein, Trans.). ICS Publications. (Original work published 1917)

Strasser, S. (1963). *Phenomenology and the human sciences: A contribution to a new scientific ideal*. Duquesne University Press.

Sullivan, H. S. (1954). *The psychiatric interview*. Norton.

Tenreiro, C. Z. (2017). *"Being" in the eye of the beholder: A phenomenological inquiry into being seen by the other* [Unpublished senior thesis]. University of Dallas.

Tomkins, L., & Eatough, V. (2013). The feel of experience: Phenomenological ideas for organizational research. *Qualitative Research in Organizations and Management, 8*(3), 258–275. https://doi.org/10.1108/QROM-04-2012-1060

Valle, R. S. (Ed.). (1998). *Phenomenological inquiry: Existential and transpersonal dimensions*. Plenum Press. https://doi.org/10.1007/978-1-4899-0125-5

Valle, R. S., & Halling, S. (Eds.). (1989). *Existential-phenomenological perspectives in psychology: Exploring the breadth and depth of human experience*. Plenum Press. https://doi.org/10.1007/978-1-4615-6989-3

van den Berg, J. H. (1972). *A different existence: Principles of phenomenological psychopathology*. Duquesne University Press.

Van Kaam, A. (1966). *Existential foundations of psychology*. Duquesne University Press.

Van Kaam, A. (1987). *Formative spirituality: Vol. 4. Scientific formation.* Crossroad.

van Manen, M. (1990). *Researching lived experience: Human science for an action sensitive pedagogy* (2nd ed.). State University of New York Press.

van Manen, M. (Ed.). (2002). *Writing in the dark: Phenomenological studies in interpretive inquiry.* Routledge.

van Manen, M. (2017). Phenomenology in its original sense. *Qualitative Health Research, 27*(6), 810–825. https://doi.org/10.1177/1049732317699381

von Eckartsberg, R. (1971). On experiential methodology. In A. Giorgi, W. F. Fischer, & R. von Eckartsberg (Eds.), *Duquesne studies in phenomenological psychology* (Vol. 1, pp. 66–79). Duquesne University Press.

von Eckartsberg, R. (1986). *Life-world experience: Existential-phenomenological research approaches in psychology.* Center for Advanced Research in Phenomenology.

Walsh, R. (2016). Evidence, argument, and phenomenology. In C. T. Fischer, R. Brooke, & L. Laubscher (Eds.), *The qualitative vision for psychology: An invitation to a human science approach* (pp. 117–132). Duquesne University Press.

Watanabe, C. K. (2014). *Finding oneself outcast in an alienating regard: A phenomenological inquiry into the experience of social exclusion* [Unpublished senior thesis]. University of Dallas.

Watson, K. L. (2016). *Spreading your wings: A phenomenological investigation of independence in early adulthood* [Unpublished senior thesis]. University of Dallas.

Wertz, F. J. (1985). Methods and findings in an empirical analysis of "being criminally victimized." In A. Giorgi (Ed.), *Phenomenology and psychological research* (pp. 155–216). Duquesne University Press.

Wertz, F. J. (2010). The method of eidetic analysis for psychology. In T. F. Cloonan & C. Thiboutot (Eds.), *The redirection of psychology: Essays in honor of Amedeo P. Giorgi* (pp. 261–278). Le Cercle Interdisciplinaire de Recherches Phénoménologiques, l'Université du Québec à Montréal et Rimouski.

Wertz, F. J., Charmaz, K., McMullen, L. M., Josselson, R., Anderson, R., & McSpadden, E. (2011). *Five ways of doing qualitative analysis: Phenomenological psychology, grounded theory, discourse analysis, narrative research, and intuitive inquiry.* Guilford Press.

Wertz, F. J., & Olbert, C. (2016). The convergence of Freud's psychoanalysis and Husserl's phenomenology on a research approach for human sciences. In C. T. Fischer, R. Brooke, & L. Laubscher (Eds.), *The qualitative vision for psychology: An invitation to a human science approach* (pp. 244–269). Duquesne University Press.

Index

A

Access questions
  developing, 23
  distinguishing research interests from,
    23–24
  formulation of, 38–40
  for sensitive subjects, 24
Allen, Woody, 7
Anger, reframing, 12–13
An-schauen (looking-at, intuiting), 36, 83
The Ape and the Sushi Master (de Waal),
  86
Approach subsection, 75

B

"Because motives"
  "in-order-to motives" vs., 15–17
  and intentionality, 13
Befragte (what is interrogated, the
  interviewee), 22, 26–27, 31
"Being seen by the other," study of,
  22–23
Bodily felt sense, 54
Bodily relation, 53
Body language, 43
Bogart, Humphrey, 7
Bracketing, 9, 80, 81

C

Capta (taken, captured), 36–37
Casablanca (film), 7
Causality, 16, 86

Choice
  and intentionality, 12–13
  sense of self as basis for, 13–14
Churchill, S. D., 29, 86
Circular temporality, 13–15
Circumstances. *See also* Situations
  ability to choose how to react in, 11–12
  coming to terms with one's, 27–28
Co-experiencing, 54
Colaizzi, P. F., 69, 87
Concentrated focusing, 54–55
Condensed general structural descriptions
  (GSDs), 69–71
Constituents, interrelationships among,
  62–63
Cooperative dialogue, interviews as, 41

D

Data
  preliminary familiarization with, 49
Data analysis. *See also* First phase;
  Second phase
  process of, 49
  in research reports, 75
Data collection, 33–46
  ethical considerations in, 33–34
  experiential approach to, 36–37
  participant selection, 35–36
  recommended procedure for, 38–45
  researcher's facilitative presence in,
    45–46
  in research reports, 75

Data-generating activities, 37–46
De Beauvoir, S., 22, 26, 62
Deep listening, 56
"Depth psychology," 8
De Waal, Frans, 86
Dilthey, W., 6, 8, 31, 54
Disciplined fascination, 54–55
Discussion section, 77
Domestic abuse, existential
    phenomenological research on,
    30–31
"Do no harm," in research, 34
Duquesne University, 4

E

Eidetic reduction, 67–68
Eidos (unity of sense), 67, 84
Ein-fühlen (to "feel" one's way "in"), 37,
    54, 80
Einfühlung (empathy), 37, 54, 80
Emotions, reframing, 12–13
Empathic dwelling, 45, 53–54
Empathy
    active practice of, 37
    in approach to data collection, 36
    as essential component of EPR, 7, 80
    in follow-up interviews, 42
Englander, M., 35
Epoché (bracketing), 9, 81
EPR. *See* Existential phenomenological
    research
Erfragte (what is asked for, the findings),
    22, 27
Ethical considerations, 33–34
Existential approach, 10–12
Existential choice, 12–13
Existential gestalts, 6
"Existential-hermeneutic" method, 4
Existential phenomenological research
    (EPR), 3–19, 79–87
    circular temporality vs. linear
        determinism, 13–15
    existential approach to the person,
        10–12
    existential choice and transcendence,
        12–13
    future directions for, 87
    as "human science" approach, 5–10
    "in-order-to motives" vs. "because
        motives," 15–17
    key features of, 17–19

limitations and weaknesses of, 86–87
methodological integrity, 81–85
in qualitative tradition, 80–81
strengths and advantages of, 85
Experiential approach, 36–37
Experimental approach, reframing, 29–30
Explanation
    as limitation in phenomenology, 86
    understanding vs., 15–17, 30–31
Explicitation, 28
Exploratory research, engaging in, 25
External validity, 83–85

F

Face-to-face follow-up interviews, 42–43
Facial expressions, 43
Facilitative presence
    in data collection, 36, 45–46
    in transformative reflections, 53–57
Familiarization with whole, 49–50
Fidelity, 82
First impressions, in data collection, 40
First-person perspective, 68–69
First phase (data analysis), 47–60
    concentrated focusing and disciplined
        fascination, 54–55
    deep listening, 56
    division of transcript into "meaning
        units," 50
    empathic dwelling, 53–54
    familiarization with whole, 49–50
    illustration of, 57–58
    intentional analysis, 56–57
    training research team for, 59–60
    transformative reflections, 51–53
Fischer, W. F., 68, 69, 71
Focusing, 6, 18, 21, 46, 47, 54, 67–68
Follow-up interviews, 40–45
Fragen (asking), 22
Frankl, Viktor, 8
Free variation in the imagination, 67–69,
    71, 84
Freud, S., 8

G

Gadamer, H. G., 83
Gefragte (what is asked about, the research
    question), 22, 26–27, 31
Geisteswissenschaft ("human science"
    approach), 5–10

General structural descriptions (GSDs), 66–71, 85
Giorgi, A., 5, 28, 35, 50, 69

H

"Hearkening," 46, 56
Heidegger, Martin
  on asking questions, 22
  on existential approach to person, 10–11
  existential-hermeneutic method of, 4
  on hearkening, 56
  on inquiry, 82
  on meaning making, 28
  on phenomenological approach, 36, 87
  on projecting self, 31
  on signification, 14–15
  on understanding, 46
Heuristic dimension, of qualitative research, 25
Human experiencing, 6
"Human sciences" (*Geisteswissenschaften*), 5–10
Husserl, Edmund
  on bodily relation, 53
  on data analysis, 67
  on intentionality, 7–8, 30
  on "natural attitude," 48
  on personal attitude, 84
  on reduction, 9–10
  on trading places, 53–54, 80
  transcendental philosophical method of, 3–4
  on unity of sense, 84

I

Idiographic findings, 66, 76
Illustrated general structural descriptions (GSDs), 69–71
Impure reflection, 15–17
Indirect questioning, 24
Individual structural descriptions (ISDs), 62–66
"In-order-to motives," 15–17
Integrity, 82
Intentional analysis, 56–57
Intentionality
  accessing, 9–10
  concept of, 7–9
  latent, 29, 57

  in purifying reflection, 17
  in research questions, 29
Internal validity, 82–83
Interrelationships, among constituents, 62–63
Interviews
  as data collection method, 37–38
  follow-up, 40–45
Introduction section, 74
Intuition
  and data collection, 36
  of essential meaning, 66–71
  and interpretation, 83
ISDs (individual structural descriptions), 62–66

K

Knowledge claims, 76, 84

L

Laing, R. D., 36–37
Languages, using participants' native, 40
Latent content, 8–9
Latent intentionality, 29, 57
Levitt, H. M., 5, 81, 82
Linear determinism
  and "because motives," 15
  circular temporality vs., 13–15
Listening, 45–46
  and bodily relation, 53
  deep, 56
Lived experience
  access questions designed to encompass, 39
  conducting research as, 73
  as criteria for participant selection, 35
  example of follow-up interview about, 43–45
  researchers bodily felt sense of, 54
  as subject of study, 21, 79
"Looking at," 28–31, 36
"Looking for," 28–31

M

Meaning
  coconstituted, from circumstances, 30
  as context dependent, 27
  elaboration of, in follow-up interviews, 40–41

and existential temporality, 13–14
finding, from lived experiences, 28
gathering, in research, 37
in intentional analysis, 56–57
intuition of essential, 66–71
in small details, 54–55
surface vs. deeper, 45–46
and transformative reflections, 51
units of, 50
Mena Ibarra, G. J., 52, 64–65, 70
Mentoring, in EPR training, 59–60
Merleau-Ponty, Maurice, 3, 8–9, 83
Methodological integrity, 81–85
Method section, 74–76
Miranda, N., 27–28
Motivational contexts or horizons, 3, 6,
   16, 18
Moustakas, C., 25, 42

N

Nach-erleben (co-experiencing), 54
Naive participants, 35
Narration, 59
Noesis (conscious act or intention), 6, 10
Noema (meaning or content of
   consciousness), 6, 10
Nonverbal communication, 43

O

Open-ended access questions, 24
Open-ended research interests, 24–25
"The Other's regard" theory, 39

P

Participants
   as coresearchers, 28
   ethical considerations for, 34
   observation of, 37
   selection of, 35–36
Passive receptivity, 45
Perceptions, 48
Phenomenological attitude, 6
Phenomenological reduction, 9–10
Phenomenon, 26–27, 47–48
Play It Again, Sam (film), 7, 8
Population, defining, 35–36
Preconceptions, 9–10
Preparation, for interviews, 41
Procedure subsection, 75–76

Psychoanalysis, 8–9
Psychological determinism, 16
Psychological hermeneutics, 31
Psychological phenomena, 26–27
Psychological retelling of story, 63, 66
Psychology as a Human Science (Giorgi), 5
Purifying reflections, 15–17
Purposive sampling, 35

Q

Qualitative research
   existential phenomenological research
     in, 80–81
   heuristic dimension of, 25
Questions
   access. *See* Access questions
   asked by researchers, 42
   indirect questioning, 24
   open-ended access, 24
   research, 22–31

R

Reducere (restore, lead back), 9–10, 57
Reduction
   example of, 58
   phenomenological, 9–10
   in second phase of data analysis, 67–68
Researcher reflexivity, 48–49
Research interests
   distinguishing from access questions,
     23–24
   in Introduction section, 74
   open-ended, 24–25
Research phenomenon, 26
Research questions, 22–31
Research report, 73–77
   Discussion section, 77
   Introduction section, 74
   Method section, 74–76
   Results section, 76
Research team, 59–60
Results section, 76
Retelling, of story, 63, 66
Ruiz de Somocurcio, D., 43

S

Sampling, 35
Sartre, Jean-Paul, 3, 11, 12, 15, 16, 26, 39
"The scene of empathy," 7

Schütz, A., 9, 15
Second person perspective, 42
Second phase (data analysis), 61–72
  general structural description, 66–71
  individual structural description,
    62–66
Sedimentation, 80
Seeing of essences (*Wesensschau*), 67
Significations, 14–15, 27, 54
Situations
  ability to choose how to react in, 11–12
  distinguishing research phenomenon
    from, 26
  psychological phenomena embedded
    within, 26–27
Specificity, in research formulation, 25
Spiegelberg, H., 59
Story, psychological retelling of, 63, 66
Structural description
  general, 66–71
  individual, 62–66
Study design, 21–31
  coming to terms with one's life
    circumstances, 27–28
  distinguishing research interests from
    access questions, 23–24
  distinguishing research phenomenon
    from situation, 26
  formulation of research question, 22–31
  indirect questioning, 24
  "looking at" vs. "looking for," 28–31
  open-ended research interests, 24–25
  psychological phenomena embedded
    within situations, 26–27
Surface meanings, 45–46
Synopses, 63, 76

T

Tabula rasa theory of knowledge, 36–37
Tenreiro, C. Z., 23, 26
Themes, 80–81
Theory of science, 5, 13, 35–36,

"Think-aloud method," 15
"Thrown projection," 11
"Trading places," 7
Transcendence, 12–13
Transcendental method, 3–4
Transcriptions
  of follow-up interviews, 42
  "meaning units" in, 50
Transformative reflections, 51–53
Trauma, studying experiences of, 34

U

Understanding (*Verstehen*), 6, 15, 30
  and empathic listening, 46
  explanations vs., 15–17, 30–31
Units of meaning, 50
Unity of sense (*eidos*), 67, 84
Universe of possible experiences, 83–85

V

Validity
  external, 83–85
  internal, 82–83
Van den Berg, J. H., 8, 62–63
Vicarious experience, 15, 39, 56, 71
Von Eckartsberg, R., 41

W

Watanabe, C. K., 11
Watson, K. L., 50
Ways of knowing, 4
Wertz, F. J., 62, 68, 81
Wesensschau (seeing of essences), 67
Workshop approach, 59–60
World of experience, 35, 84
Written descriptions
  as data collection method, 38
  in follow-up interviews, 41–42
  in research reports, 76
Written notes, of researchers, 51

About the Author

Scott D. Churchill, PhD, began studying existential phenomenology in 1969 at Bucknell University and continued his studies at Duquesne University, where he earned his doctorate in "clinical phenomenological psychology" in 1984. He began his professional career at the University of Dallas in 1981, where he currently holds the position of professor, having earlier served as department chair and founding director of the master's programs in psychology.

A fellow of the American Psychological Association (APA), he has served as editor-in-chief of *The Humanistic Psychologist* since 2006 and is currently president of APA's Society for Theoretical and Philosophical Psychology. He has also served on the APA Council of Representatives and as president of the Society for Humanistic Psychology (APA Division 32), as well as editor of *Methods: A Journal for Human Science*, while also participating on numerous editorial boards both here and abroad. He is a founding member of the International Human Science Research Conference, the Society for Qualitative Inquiry in Psychology, and the Interdisciplinary Coalition of North American Phenomenologists.

Dr. Churchill has presented papers, workshops, and invited addresses at professional conferences around the world, including Italy, Norway, Sweden, Denmark, Germany, Taiwan, Malaysia, Canada, England, India, and Australia. He has authored numerous articles and book chapters in the fields of phenomenological research methodology, empathy studies, human–bonobo communication, and second-person perspectivity. He has developed and taught well over 100 courses in phenomenological psychology, hermeneutics, depth psychology, projective techniques, ecopsychology, primate studies, and cinema studies.

Dr. Churchill was awarded the Mike Arons and E. Mark Stern Award for Outstanding Lifetime Service to the Society for Humanistic Psychology and the Charlotte and Karl Bühler Award for Outstanding and Lasting Contribution to Humanistic Psychology from APA Division 32 (Society for Humanistic Psychology) and the Steve Harrist Distinguished Service Award from Division 24 (Society for Theoretical and Philosophical Psychology). He was also named a Minnie Stevens Piper Professor for excellence in teaching. Locally, Dr. Churchill is a fellow of the Dallas Institute of Humanities and Culture and senior film and performing arts critic for the Irving Community Television Network.

About the Series Editors

Clara E. Hill, PhD, earned her doctorate at Southern Illinois University in 1974. She started her career in 1974 as an assistant professor in the Department of Psychology, University of Maryland, College Park, and is currently there as a professor.

She is the president-elect of the Society for the Advancement of Psychotherapy, and has been the president of the Society for Psychotherapy Research, the editor of the *Journal of Counseling Psychology*, and the editor of *Psychotherapy Research*.

Dr. Hill was awarded the Leona Tyler Award for Lifetime Achievement in Counseling Psychology from Division 17 (Society of Counseling Psychology) and the Distinguished Psychologist Award from Division 29 (Society for the Advancement of Psychotherapy) of the American Psychological Association, the Distinguished Research Career Award from the Society for Psychotherapy Research, and the Outstanding Lifetime Achievement Award from the Section on Counseling and Psychotherapy Process and Outcome Research of the Society of Counseling Psychology. Her major research interests are helping skills, psychotherapy process and outcome, training therapists, dream work, and qualitative research.

She has published more than 250 journal articles, 80 chapters in books, and 17 books (including *Therapist Techniques and Client Outcomes: Eight Cases of Brief Psychotherapy*; *Helping Skills: Facilitating Exploration, Insight, and Action*; and *Dream Work in Therapy: Facilitating Exploration, Insight, and Action*).

Sarah Knox, PhD, joined the faculty of Marquette University in 1999 and is a professor in the Department of Counselor Education and Counseling Psychology in the College of Education. She earned her doctorate at the

University of Maryland and completed her predoctoral internship at The Ohio State University.

Dr. Knox's research has been published in a number of journals, including *The Counseling Psychologist*, *Counselling Psychology Quarterly*, *Journal of Counseling Psychology*, *Psychotherapy*, *Psychotherapy Research*, and *Training and Education in Professional Psychology*. Her publications focus on the psychotherapy process and relationship, supervision and training, and qualitative research. She has presented her research both nationally and internationally and has provided workshops on consensual qualitative research at both U.S. and international venues.

She currently serves as coeditor-in-chief of *Counselling Psychology Quarterly* and is also on the publication board of Division 29 (Society for the Advancement of Psychotherapy) of the American Psychological Association. Dr. Knox is a fellow of Division 17 (Society of Counseling Psychology) and Division 29 of the American Psychological Association.